THE BEST OF
BILL VAUGHAN

THE BEST OF BILL VAUGHAN

Edited and Compiled by
Kirk W. Vaughan and Robert W. Butler

Independence Press, Drawer HH,
Independence, MO 64055

Library of Congress Cataloging in Publication Data

Vaughan, Bill.
    The best of Bill Vaughan.

    1. American wit and humor. I.   Vaughan, Kirk W.
II.   Butler, Robert W., 1948-   III. Title.
PN6162.V348   818'.5'407   79-20169
ISBN 0-8309-0261-9

Printed in the United States of America

To Bob Busby
Bill Vaughan's longtime friend,
co-worker, and admirer,
whose selfless research made this book possible.

ACKNOWLEDGMENTS

The authors wish to gratefully acknowledge permission to reprint excerpts from Mr. Vaughan's three books, *Sorry I Stirred It*, 1964; *Bird Thou Never Wert*, 1962; and *Half the Battle*, 1963, published by Simon and Schuster, 1230 Avenue of the Americas, New York, N.Y. 10020.

The authors also gratefully acknowledge permission to reprint material from the *Kansas City Star*, published by the Kansas City Star Company, 1729 Grand Avenue, Kansas City, Missouri 64108.

INTRODUCTION

A Bill Vaughan book always is an occasion of joy.

But this is the first one published posthumously. So please, let me for a minute remember the Bill Vaughan we knew at the *Kansas City Star*, the columnist and associate editor who made us proud to be part of the same newspaper. Over the years a lot of talented people came to the *Star*, partly because of the quality that radiated from Bill Vaughan's Starbeams column.

I don't know that his gift needs analysis any more than does the configuration of colors on a blue jay's wing. (Bill often noted that nothing is less amusing than a sincere attempt to analyze why people laugh.) His gentle genius is there; it is beautiful and you are thankful for it. Maybe it is in the mesh of words that can so magically express, in a few syllables, a familiar happiness, an old sorrow, an emotion common to us all. Like Sherlock Holmes, he made it look easy until you tried it.

Those who worked with him every day knew that the fluid Vaughan sentences came from an amazing depth of knowledge, a tremendous store of reading that grew almost nightly. Ideas and words seemed to click routinely into place for Bill Vaughan. They were drawn from a great pool of information and a massive intelligence.

Sometimes I think that a fundamental secret always was out there in the open for us to see every day—his innate kindness and instinctive sympathy. Like that of most writers, his ego was exceedingly healthy. In conversation he could zap the pompous and the phony with a kind of zestful glee that seldom made print. He tended to give short shrift to poseurs and journalistic hobbyists. Most of his co-workers counted it a high compliment to be insulted by Vaughan, editorial writers especially.

His essential human characteristics were compassion and charity. The man had an unbelievable work load. Yet time after time he would listen patiently for an hour or more and laugh at feeble witticisms from an admirer who would drop in out of the sky on the busiest day. Or spend time with a syndicate salesman on his weary rounds, peddling columns and cartoons that both Bill and the salesman knew wouldn't be bought. "It's a very tough job," he would say. He always had time.

Maybe it takes a complex, sometimes contradictory nature to create such writing. If he could read this he would say that it is best to beware of editorial writers bearing clumsy affection, and wickedly deflate these words.

We still miss him.

James W. Scott
Editorial Page Editor
The *Kansas City Star* and *Times*

JANUARY

The Resolutions Consultant

Busy men, which includes most of us, no longer select their own Christmas gifts. That is done for them by a gift consultant. Nor do they make out their own internal revenue forms. The little tax man does that. They do not even decide what to do with their money, if any, after they die. An estate planner does that for them.

With this in mind, it strikes me that there is an obvious gap waiting to be filled. Why should a man be expected to take the time to make his own New Year's resolutions?

The need is for a Resolutions Consultant. He or she would be a highly trained specialist. Obviously it would not do to get one's resolutions off the rack, so to speak. They must be custom tailored.

"Hi, there, I'm your Resolutions Consultant. May I be of assistance? Have a delicious mint and relax."

"Well, I would like to make some resolutions, but I haven't made any since I was 16 years old and, well, things—"

"Have changed since then? Of course, and now you want something more up-to-date in resolutions. About how many did you have in mind?"

"How do they come?"

"I beg your pardon."

"I mean do you have to have five or ten or a dozen, something like that? Or could you just have one or two?"

The Resolutions Consultant would explain that you can make as many or as few as you want.

"However," he would continue, "the best professional thinking is that to make fewer than five is a mistake. There is a certain breakage problem, you know. Occasionally a client will come back and express disappointment if he has broken all his resolutions by the first of March. For this reason we suggest a few spares."

"I can see that," the client will nod. "Is there any guarantee that resolutions will last the full twelve months?"

"Not really, although we have developed a few techniques. A very popular resolution, for example, is not to spend all next January first in front of the tube watching football games."

"That sounds like a pretty tough resolution to keep."

"Yes, but the beauty of it is that it's impossible to break it until next New Year's Day. It's about the only item on which we give a twelve-month warranty."

"All right, put me down for that. By the way, is all this going to cost me a lot of money?"

"On the contrary. We are like your tax adviser. Our modest fee more than pays for itself in savings, because most resolutions are to stop doing something, and doing almost anything costs money."

"Like resolving to quit smoking."

"Yes, except that I don't really recommend that. Frankly it's a sort of drab, commonplace resolution. A man in your position needs something with a little more class. Ten years ago, perhaps, a man could get some attention by announcing that he had resolved to give up tobacco. But now it's yawnsville."

12

"I was going to resolve to lose weight. But I suppose that's in the same category?"

"No, interestingly enough, dieting resolutions are not only popular but continue to be a prestige item. Some of our top clients seem to feel that being overweight in a distressed economy carries a certain amount of distinction."

After a few more exchanges, the filling out of a questionnaire, and the payment of the fee, the busy man can go about his affairs. In due time he will receive his individually prepared resolutions, bound in a simulated leather folder with his name in gold leaf (at a slight extra charge).

He can then put it away unopened, secure in the knowledge that society has relieved him of yet another troublesome chore.

Confessions of a Whiffle-Remover

Getting older tends to perfect the character, so that it becomes increasingly difficult to find any bad habits to give up.

It made me very happy, therefore, to discover the other day that I was doing something that I might just as well not do any more. So I am making a resolution as follows:

Resolved, that I will not tear the whiffles from the edges of postage stamps.

Whiffle may not be the exact philatelic term for which I am groping, but that's what I call them. They are little strips of paper that cling to the tops, sides, or bottoms of stamps that come from the outer rows of a sheet.

According to their position, they may be referred to as the superior or overhead whiffle, the inferior or bottom whiffle, and the lateral (sinister) or lateral (dexter) whiffle.

Actually, there is no reason for removing the whiffle before affixing the stamp to the envelope. The whiffle does not impair the legality of the stamp or its efficiency in conveying the letter from place to place.

I have never heard of anyone strangling on a whiffle while licking a stamp. As a matter of fact, if you like the taste of stamps the whiffle adds just a soupcon more, sort of a mucilaginous lagniappe.

Still, I am a whiffle-remover. Don't ask why. For some reason, I seem to attract bewhiffled stamps; rarely does a whiffleless one come my way. And before I use it I tear off the whiffle. This takes time. Especially if it is a double whiffle. Obviously, the corner stamps on the sheet are double-whifflers—superior-lateral (dexter), for example.

Although I have never exactly clocked the time it takes to dewhiffle a stamp, it takes longer than you might think. The whiffle is hard to get hold of and remove without tearing the stamp itself. It takes a delicate touch. The carrying of whiffle tweezers might help some, but they are hard to find in the stores.

Admittedly, stamp dewhiffling has its compensations—it's a lot like smoking. It eases nervous tension the way a cigarette does, gives you something to do with your hands, helps relieve boredom during long waits at the dentist's office, etc.

But, like smoking, it is a messy habit. What do you do with the whiffle after you have removed it? It's as big a problem as a cigarette butt. You can't throw it on the floor if you are a basically neat person. And if you put it in your pocket or trouser cuff, like you do with olive seeds at a buffet supper, what happens eventually is that you have a pocket or a trouser cuff full of whiffles.

Whiffles are useless. Even if you saved enough of them to stuff a pillow you wouldn't want to do it.

But the big thing is the waste of time. As I said earlier, I don't know exactly how long it takes to remove a whiffle, but it must be several seconds at least. For a heavy mailer, over a year's time, it would add up.

In the time saved by not removing whiffles from stamps I expect to be able to straighten out a lot of paper clips.

❖❖❖❖❖

The Interview

Q: Well, coach, are your Behemoths in good condition for the annual Fudge Bowl New Year's Day classic which is expected to jam the stadium to capacity besides entertaining fans across the land via the nationwide teevy?

A: Thank you, Ed. First of all I might say that our team is not the Behemoths. That is the other team, I think. We are the Basset Hounds, as is well known by fans across the land who will be watching us in the Fudge Bowl classic on New Year's Day either in person or through the nationwide teevy. It is nice to be here, Ed.

Q: Thank you, coach, and I do want to apologize for calling your team the Behemoths instead of the Beagle Hounds.

A: Basset Hounds.

Q: Basset Hounds. It's just that there are so many bowl games this year and I'm not the regular sports man around here anyway and I got stuck with this interview because the regular sports man—but never mind about him. Anyway, coach, are your charges in good condition?

A: My charges are in terrible condition, due to my wife's going crazy and buying everything in the stores. Ha. Ha.

Q: By charges, coach, I mean your players.

A: I was being light, Ed. But seriously, Ed, are you asking about the condition of my players?

Q: Yes, coach. I think we would all like to have a little insight into whether All-America Honorable Mention, the rifle-armed and game little quarterback Digby Dabbs, will be at his rifle-armed peak.

A: Ed, let me say this about Digby. He is a fine boy and he will give 100 percent.

Q: Well, coach, the fans will be glad to get this good news about Digby Dabbs.

A: What good news? He's a fine boy who will give 100 percent, but he has a broken leg.

Q: Oh, well, uh, coach, about New Year's Day. Would you care to pick a winner?

A: Yes, I would care to pick a winner.

Q: Well:

A: Well, what?

Q: Well, so pick a winner.

A: O.K. Missouri in the Orange Bowl.

Q: No, no, coach. I mean a winner in the Fudge Bowl.

A: Frankly, Ed, between us and the Behemoths I don't think there will be a winner in the Fudge Bowl.

Q: Ah, speaking of the Behemoths—have you scouted them or seen their game movies?

A: We have seen their game movies and, frankly, they are the worst movies since Lionel Atwill in *The Vampire Bat.* You couldn't tell the good guys from the bad guys. Terrible movies. Half the time I didn't even know where the ball was.

Q: What kind of team do the Behemoths have?

A: Well, Ed, let me say this—they play hard-nosed football.

Q: What kind?

A: Hard-nosed.

Q: What does that mean exactly?

A: I don't know. I read it in the newspaper.

Q: What sort of strategy have you planned?

A: We will play soft-nosed football, Ed.

Q: Soft-nosed?

A: Yes, everybody else has played hard-nosed football this

year. We figure that if we play soft-nosed football it will sort of catch the Behemoths by surprise.

Q: And well it might.

A: I'm the only coach left in the game who still teaches soft-nosed football, but I think the others will come back to it.

Q: The pendulum—

A: Will swing. Yes.

Q: Speaking of coaches, how about Coach Pug Underslung of the Behemoths?

A: Well, there's this to be said about the Behemoths—they play hard-nosed football, but they are very poorly coached. What's the matter, Ed? You look pale.

Q: Twenty-five years in this business, and you're the first coach I ever heard say that the opposing team was badly coached.

A: Don't get me wrong, Ed. As a man, as a brother-in-law, Underslung leaves a lot to be desired, but as a coach he's a mess. A hard-nosed mess.

Q: Do you have any parting tips for the fans, coach?

A: Yes. Watch the Rose Bowl.

❖❖❖❖

The Facts of Life

"Daddy!"

"Yes?"

"What does this picture mean? This picture in the magazine. See, this man is standing there in the doorway holding a cup, and he is talking to this lady, and what is he saying?"

"Well, this guy has this cup and he says to the lady, 'My wife would like to borrow a cup of . . . a cup of . . . a cup of . . . .'"

"Why does he keep saying 'a cup of' like that?"

"Well, this is a funny picture, you understand. It's what they call a cartoon. It's just to be funny and make people laugh."

"Is it funny to keep on saying 'a cup of'?"

"No, but—"

"A cup of, cup of, cupuvcupuvcupuv. . . ."

"All right, all right. You don't understand. This lady that he is trying to borrow the sugar from, or coffee, or whatever, well, she's quite a sexy, uh, a very pretty lady, and this fellow is looking at her and forgets what he came for and. . . ."

"Why?"

"Now look, I will tolerate almost anything except 'why?' It makes us sound like one of those families on television. Anyway, this is for grown-ups. Go on back and read 'Skoojie the Skunk' some more."

"I want to hear about this picture."

"O.K. Well, that's the first picture. The man can't remember what he was supposed to borrow because the woman is so—pretty. Well, then, in the next picture the man is gone and here is his wife, and she is saying, 'Flour.'"

"Hum."

"It's funny, see. The man's wife sees that her husband thinks the woman is pretty and can't remember what it was he was supposed to borrow, so she comes out and says, 'Flour.'"

"I think the wife is prettier than the woman. She's fatter."

"Yes, but she's not quite so—"

"Quite so what?"

"Never mind. Go on back to 'Skoojie the Skunk.'"

"No, I want to look at some more pictures. Here's one. What's this mean?"

"Hm. Well, here is a man and his wife sitting at a table in a restaurant. And. . . ."

"Daddy?"

"Yes?"

"Why do men and their wives always look so mad at each other in these pictures?"

"Because it's funny."

"But when you and mommy look mad it's not..."

"Never mind. Underneath it, here, this is what the man is saying...."

"How do you know the man's talking?"

"Because he has his mouth open."

"But there isn't any bubble coming out of his mouth to show who's talking, like in 'Peanuts.'"

"That's because this isn't a newspaper strip. This is a magazine cartoon."

"Well, why do people in newspapers have bubbles coming out of their mouths and people in magazines don't?"

"It's because of the paper. This paper is much smoother than the paper the newspaper is printed on. Does that answer your question?"

"Yes."

"Do you feel all right?"

"Why?"

"Nothing. It's just that I've never known you to give up so easily. Anyway, the man says, 'Oh, go ahead and eat it—it wouldn't dare disagree with you.'"

"Why are you groaning, daddy?"

"That gag. I kicked the slats out of my cradle laughing at that one."

"Did you really?"

"Sure, that's the oldest gag in the world. Where are you going? Bring back that magazine."

"I'm going up to read it to the baby. I want to see him kick the slats out."

"Hey, wait...I was reading that! There's nothing else to read. Except...oh, well.

"'Skoojie was a little skunk. And all the other forest animals...'!"

❖❖❖❖

There's No Place Like Home

Mostly I understand what goes on in the movie and teevy drama because both are tailored for the nominal mind. But there are two scenes I have never figured out. Or rather it's basically one scene, but it differs somewhat according to the particular role of the sexes.

It is the one where he leaves her or she leaves him. In the first case he says, "I am going to my club."

Many an impressionable husband has tried this, storming out the front door into the rain, only to remember, while he is waiting at the bus stop, that the only club he belongs to is the National Geographic Society, which is in far-off Washington and, as far as he knows, doesn't have a spare bed. Being a husband, he has a total of fifty-three cents in his pocket and he has to squiggle back into the house in a rather wet and chastened manner.

Also, in these romances, the husband may pack a bag. Where does he find the suitcase? We are never shown. We just cut to the scene where he has the suitcase on the bed and is filling it with socks and shirts out of a dresser drawer.

Come on, now. You know where the suitcases are in the average home? They are in the attic and if a husband wants to run away he has to go up there in the indescribable mess and crack his head on the rafters, which is why lots of marriages stay together. If he does find the suitcase, it is full of his children's old arithmetic papers.

And where is he getting all that stuff to pack? The socks,

ordinarily, are hanging in the basement to dry and the shirts are at the laundry. If a man has the kind of home that he can get out of in five minutes, all neatly packed, and if he can afford a club to sleep in, he's got the kind of setup he'd be a fool to leave in the first place.

Things are even more unreal when it's the wife who is skipping out on the husband.

The exit line is usually something like "Sorry, Cedric, but it just won't work. Heaven and Mother know I've tried. Sam is waiting for me in a taxicab."

She walks out. Do you catch the unreality of it? No instructions. No wife can go visit her sister in Des Moines for a weekend without leaving behind field orders more complete than those for the Normandy invasion. I can't think that this infatuation for a mere Sam is going to change feminine nature that much.

It would be more likely to go something like this:

"Sorry, Cedric. It won't work. Remember Mathilda's dancing lesson tomorrow, and she goes to the orthodontist's on Tuesday. I've tried, Cedric, but it's too much. That stuff in the plastic pan on the third shelf of the refrigerator is the dog's food. The leftover hash is wrapped in foil in the freezer. Remember if you don't put out a note for the milkman he'll leave two bottles of milk and you won't need that much now that I'll be with Sam.

"Oh, and if Miss Flange from the upholsterer's calls, tell her to go ahead with the green slipcover. Hadn't you better write this down? Good-bye, Cedric, we had our laughs but it wasn't enough. I think the mayonnaise is rancid—you'd better throw it out—and send your gray suit to the cleaners."

She leaves. The disconsolate husband looks out the window. She sticks her head out of the cab and yells, "Tell the Porters we can't make it next Friday night unless you want to go by yourself. Wear a red tie with your blue suit and get

Mrs. Damply to sit with Mathilda."

Cedric slumps into a chair. Minutes pass. The telephone rings. It's his wife.

"Sam and I are at the airport," she says. "When you open the refrigerator door, a little light may come on; don't let it frighten you."

An hour later she's home. Taking off with Sam just doesn't seem to be worth all the advance planning.

That's the way things happen in real life up and down every block, but you'd never know it from the silver screen or the giant eye.

Ah, Yes, I Remember It Well...

For some reason there seems to be more nostalgia in my set than there was, say, twenty-five years ago.

People sit around and they say, "Boy, do you remember licorice whips and those little sugar hearts with mottoes on them and sleeve garters?"

And somebody else says, "Boy, I sure remember the bejabers out of those items you mention, and also fifteen-cent Rocket baseballs and John Bunny and 'The Bungles' and climbing up on the back step of the ice wagon."

And everybody starts remembering Chalmers and the Apperson Jack-Rabbit and Eppa Jephtha Rixie and J-Ham Lewis and how good homemade peach ice cream tasted when you got to lick the paddle as a reward for turning the crank.

And people remember long underwear and McGuffey's Readers and Irving Aaronson and his Commanders and cat-whisker radios and mumblety-peg.

Well, some of this stuff I remember and some I don't. I

remember throwing a golf ball against the concrete steps and every time you caught it, why, that was a man on base, and if it hit the edge of the step that was a home run and—but it was pretty complicated. I'd have to show you.

But I lack the total recall that other people have.

Or seem to have. Do they really remember all those things? Nobody ever says they don't remember something. Not even women will admit it, even though the remembering makes them about twenty years older than they are.

When it comes to nostalgia, the great American pride in being young seems to break down. Everybody wants to say they remember home brew and celluloid collars, Tom Swift and Milton Sills.

Lately I have started testing my theory that people don't really remember the things they say they do.

I'll say something like "Boy, do you remember how swell it used to feel early in the morning when you'd go out in your bare feet and walk on the barbed wire and smell the new-mown string beans?"

And everybody says that yes, yes, they remember that very well and rush on to a memory of their own.

Or I will say, "Hey, do you remember those octagonal pink penny candies that were full of strychnine?" and they will clap their hands and say indeed, indeed, they remember them well.

I will ask, "Do you remember when we used to wear yellow slickers with crazy jokes written on them and dance the minuet?"

"Do you remember the fireworks when General Benedict Arnold came to town?"

"Do you remember the early days of radio with Mozart beating out his own stuff on the eighty-eight?"

"Do you remember when hand-knit carburetors were all the rage and all the girls wore porte cocheres?"

"Boy, how about the time they let out school when Walter Damrosch hit 63 home runs?"

"Do you remember when no home was complete without an Isotta-Fraschini in the front parlor and no nice girl spoke English?"

Yes, yes, indeed, indeed, everybody cries, and they are not even interrupted in their outpouring of rememberings about peekaboo blouses and horse cars and the St. Louis Browns.

In fact, at the end of an evening, they often seek me out to say they don't see how I can remember all those things which they might almost have forgotten if I hadn't reminded them.

Locker Room Blues

The lady who doesn't understand football was depressed by the Super Bowl. She said it was a punk show.

"Well, of course," I said, "there were those long minutes when nothing happened except the exchange of punts."

"That was O.K.," she said. "I like punts. I used to go with a punter in college. He explained it to me. And the thing about punts is that you can see them and there is not a lot of that handing the ball around where you can't tell what's going on. I consider that sort of thing very tacky."

"I suppose it must be admitted," I said, "that it wasn't a very artistic production. After all, a game with all those fumbles and interceptions. . ."

"The popovers." She nodded wisely. "I adore the popovers, when one player takes the ball away from another. They are kind of cute when they're mad, stamping their feet and all. I ' like popovers almost as much as punts."

"The technical expression, I believe, is turnovers," I suggested.

"Whatever," she said.

"But," I said, "if you like punts and thrill to evenly matched ineptness, then this should have been your kind of game. After all, it was close right down to the final gun. It almost went into sudden death."

"Kindly do not use that expression, sudden death," she said. "Maybe sudden injury would be all right, but sudden death sounds morbid, don't you think?"

"Well, anyway, when O'Brien split the uprights, as the announcers say, sudden death was avoided."

"And a good thing, too," she said.

"Because of the morbidity?"

"Well, that, of course," she said, "but mainly because it would have made the game longer and I was just sitting through it to get to the best part."

"Best part?"

"Sure," she said. "In the locker rooms afterward where everybody is pouring champagne over everybody else and bouncing the coach up and down, and throwing assistant coaches into the showers. And people are yelling they're No. 1 and jumping up on tables and waving bottles around."

"You think that's the best part?"

"Of course," replied the lady who doesn't understand football. "The rest of it you can just nod through. All that stuff about third downs being crucial and running at their strength and the strong safety on the weak side. That's plain dull."

"The only reason for putting up with it at all is so you can enjoy the locker room, with some big kid saying, 'Naw, they didn't show us nothing we wasn't expecting' and dumping a bottle of champagne on the announcer's head?"

"Yes, which is why this Super Bowl is a bummer."

25

"That's right," I said. "They didn't have any of that this time. It was much more dignified. Mr. Rozelle's idea, I suppose. After all, the sport is big enough now to have dignity."

"Dignity," she scoffed. "If I want dignity I can go watch Eric Sevareid."

"Still," I said, "I thought it was nice where, instead of all that horseplay, they introduced the players' wives. Even women who don't understand football should have liked that."

"Who needs wives?" she snorted. "I look at wives all day. We got a six hundred dollar color TV I should see more wives? I want wives on TV I can watch 'Secret Storm.'"

"The times are changing," I offered lamely.

"Too true," she snapped. "There's no tradition any more. You get a great tradition like champagne shampoos which we average nonfans look forward to each year, and all of a sudden they scrap it and put in dignity and wives. No wonder nobody trusts the networks. Anyway, I bet it's not dignity; it's just that they're too chintzy to buy the champagne."

"Maybe you're right," I conceded.

"Of course I am," said the lady who doesn't understand football. "If they weren't going to show the champagne-pouring in the great American tradition they should have warned us in advance so we wouldn't have wasted a whole afternoon watching that stupid game."

She is a lady of strong views.

❖❖❖❖

Hang-Ups

You'd think that a man with a newly papered room in his house would be a happy man, but that is not the case—not my case anyway. The paper looks fine, but the room doesn't look much better because of all the pictures stacked on a chair.

These pictures used to hang on those walls. We put them up whenever we felt like it, or wherever there was an old hole, gouge, scratch, crack, mysterious stain or bit of childish graffiti to cover up. Whanging nails into those old walls was a matter of no concern at all.

But now there is a failure of nerve. The walls are so pristine in their unblemished purity that driving the first nail seems almost like an act of sacrilege.

All the near and dear are sort of holding back, waiting for somebody else to put up the first picture. Once the ice has been broken or, more aptly, the plaster shattered, everyone can pick up hammer and nails with glad cries and get the rest of the pictures up.

It's the first one that is causing the hang-up. A hang-up on hanging up? It happens.

What is required is a commitment, a major decision that is not easy to make. If the picture is put up in the wrong place it will be there forever, or until the end of the mortgage, whichever comes first, as a silent rebuke.

And believe me, there are a lot more wrong places in a room to hang a picture than there are right ones. Those knowledgeable in the esoterics of decor say, of some of my pictures, that there is no right place to hang them, unless it might be on the inside of a closet door. I don't agree with them and I am determined to get those pictures back up.

I have even held the nail against the wall and drawn back the hammer. But my arm refuses to bring it down on nail and thumb as required. It starts to shake and I have to sit down for a while.

I have tried to persuade myself that it might be a good idea to put the first picture in the wrong place deliberately. Operating under this theory, I tell myself, the tension would be relieved. Since one picture in the wrong place had already ruined everything, putting the rest of them up would be no strain at all, and a certain higgledy-piggledy charm might be achieved.

But I haven't been able to convince myself, let alone anybody else, that this is a wise idea.

The way I see it there isn't much of any way to win. If I hang the picture wrong I go down among family and friends as a rotten picture-hanger and a wall-spoiler. On the other hand one doesn't want to be known as a man who is too cowardly to drive one little old nail.

There are other problems beside the pictures. There are worries about who is to be the first to jam the corner of a chair into the wall or put a greasy thumbprint on it. The temptation is to do something like that deliberately so that everyone can relax.

It's like the first dandelion of the spring, which seems like a calamity. After a couple of hundred have put in their appearance you quit bothering about them.

Some sort of basic law of human nature makes people, or me anyway, nervous in the presence of anything that is new and free from flaws. A familiar example is the new motorcar. How carefully we drive it until someone (someone else naturally) dents the first fender. It is a traumatic experience, but after that we are more relaxed at the wheel, and probably better drivers because of it.

Until the new hat has fallen on the restaurant floor and been stepped on, we are apprehensively conscious of its perfection. Only after it is beat up a little can we really begin to enjoy it.

The same thing goes for the new suit, until the pipe ashes have burned the first hole in it.

A friend suggests I could drive that nail if I took a drink

first. But that would be false courage. No, I am going to do it cold turkey. Resolutely. Soon.

But not today.

❖❖❖❖

Expired.. . .

Let me tell you, folks, this is a world of sadness. It isn't all roses and riots. There is the darkness as well as the sunlight. In the midst of life we may receive the word which clutches at our hearts with icy fingers. It was a plain envelope in the mail, and it seems odd that the postman could have brought it, blithely, whistling as he walked, blissfully ignorant of its dread contents.

Tears blurred my eyes as I read:

"Dear Subscriber: Your address above is made with the little metal stamp which has brought you the *Reader's Digest* every month.

"But your subscription has expired.

"It seems a shame to remove your stencil from the good company it is now keeping. In the same file with it are the stencils of Henry Kissinger, Helen Hayes, Tennessee Williams, Billy Graham, and thousands of other distinguished persons.

"We don't believe that you want us to destroy this little stencil—the last link between you and the continued visits of the stimulating, significant, and enduring articles gleaned from the world of current literature."

It is quite dark now; I am sitting alone in the living room. Suddenly I gaze at the empty bottle in my hand. With a curse I throw it into the fireplace. That is not the solution. This thing must be faced. It is not for myself that I am afraid. But the little home, the little family. The ones who trust and love me. How long will it be before the neighbors know? And the children, in their thoughtless cruelty—will they be whispering behind my child's back, "His father's little stencil is no longer keeping good company"?

How could I have been such a blind fool? To let my subscription expire! To desert that little metal stamp which has done so much for me!

My face is buried in my hands. Where to turn? What hope can there be for the future? There is no hope.

I am resigned, however. I wait here quite calmly now in the silent room, the dark room. They will be coming soon. I don't know what it will be like, but I can imagine.

The public humiliation. As I stand by, head bowed, my little metal stencil is removed from the files and tossed into a pot of molten metal. Tennessee Williams turns his back. Henry Kissinger stands rigid but the telltale whiteness around the lips bespeaks the iron control he is forced to exert.

A last look at these old companions, a half wave which they ignore, and I turn and trudge away.

Why don't they come? I am ready for the final degradation. Somewhere the little family can find another home under an assumed name, while I wander the earth alone, homeless, reading copies of *Playboy* at drugstore magazine racks, sinking lower and lower, the old familiar path—*True Stories*, *TV Guide*, down, down. But on snowy Christmas Eves I will stand outside the bright, modern-type home of my ex-loved ones and look in through the holly-decked windows at the scene within. The brightly lighted tree, the mother slowly turning the pages of *Reader's Digest*, reading aloud the stimulating, significant, and enduring articles.

Will they ever, between "Life in These United States" and "The Most Unforgettable Character I've Met," pause to think of one who loved and failed them long ago?

FEBRUARY

Missoura-e-i-o-u?

When a man sets up a certain number of principles by which to live, anything that happens to him for varying from strict adherence thereto serves him right. Among my strict rules is never to get into an argument with a person who not only doesn't know what he is talking about but has no way of knowing that he doesn't know. A man in this condition will, inevitably, draw to his side of the question the unreasoning majority of mankind.

Once I allowed myself to depart from this sensible conduct in attempting to do a favor for a wandering carpetbagger who also happened to be an old friend. His name is Martin Quigley and he is editor of *Midwest Motorist*, the organ of the Auto Club of Missouri. He is from Minnesota or some such place and I thought he would appreciate knowing how to pronounce the name of the state in which he works and to which I first introduced him forty years ago.

He called the grand old state "Missouree," which is plain wrong, and I told him so. I did not admonish him, because I think it is rather amusing to live in a state which has difficulty pronouncing itself.

Still, right is right, and friendship is friendship, so I quietly explained that the state whose Auto Club magazine he purported to edit is Mizzoura.

Rule No. 2: Never play with the other man's cards.

So I violated that one as well when he suggested a debate in his magazine, with a poll to be conducted among his readers and their ballots to be counted by his staff, on the proper pronunciation of Missouri.

I wrote a calm and well-reasoned argument, while Quigley argued strictly ad hominem, accusing me of living in a better neighborhood as a child than he did. I don't quite see the relevance, except that my boyhood was spent in Missouri and his wasn't. He also sought to cover up his lack of bona fides as a Missourian by claiming that his Great-Aunt Emma or some such had been blown up at the battle of Pilot Knob.

Naturally the result of the poll was 60 percent for the hog-calling Missouree and 40 percent for the euphonious and proper Mizzoura.

The *Midwest Motorist* printed many letters on both sides of the question, I'll give them that. I also received a fair number of communications from men of stature and perception, also a few from pompous elocution students, who disagreed with me.

Missouri was intended by God and the early settlers to be pronounced Mizzoura. Then along came the elocution teachers who thought Missouree sounded more elegant.

The proof of the classroom taint on Missouree is that people write they were taught it in school. Now in real Missouri schools, they didn't teach how to pronounce the state any more than they taught sex. They figured it was something you either knew or you didn't and probably never would get quite right.

I go back to Eugene Field, who wrote in 1889, "He lives in Mizzoura, where the people are so set . . . in ante-bellum notions that they vote for Jackson yet." (That's not Scoop Jackson.)

I take my stand with former Governor Guy B. Park when he said in 1933: "I've lived in Missouri all my life and I never heard any true Missourian pronounce the name in any other way but 'Mizzourah.'" The "rah," I'll admit, is a little strong. Actually that final "i" is more like the "a" in sofa. Although people who say, "Missouree" probably say "sofee."

I salute Frank Luther Mott who said that "the almost invariable pronunciation of old-timers in this state, and of most Missouri leaders, is 'Muhzooruh.'"

Much of the mischief originated with the revered Walter Williams, who edited a newspaper in that hotbed of culture, Columbia, and came out for "ee." To make it worse he later founded a School of Journalism which spread the heresy, especially since the prestige of the school brought in many outsiders who had no very clear idea where they were.

The state's present governor is sound on pronunciation. One of my correspondents is perhaps extreme in saying he would never vote for politicians who used the "ee" ending on the theory that they might be equally wrong on the other and possibly more important matters.

The *Midwest Motorist's* poll indicates regional variation in the way Missouri is said, with the Eastern half stronger on "ee" and the Western going for "a" or "uh."

I do not wish to get too personal, but I grew up in the great city of St. Louis and its environs (one of which Quigley, the same man who accuses me of elitism, calls a ghetto), was city editor of a paper in the great city of Springfield in the southwest part of the state, and, furthermore, my father was born in the northwest part of the state. And in none of these places did any of my kin vary from "Mizzoura."

I have pictures of old, white-bearded men sitting under the greens on the family farm in Bridgeton, Missouri, and I would not envy any Minnesotan who walked among them bleating about "Missouri-*ee*."

The beautiful part about those of us who know how to pronounce Missouri is the well-nigh saintly patience and tolerance we show toward those who don't.

I am further buoyed by the thought that, in matters of this kind, whatever the majority thinks is probably wrong. Since radio and TV people are pretty close to unanimous on the screeched "ee" I figure that they will drive Mizzoura out eventually, there being a Gresham's law that bad pronunciation drives out good. It is an honor to fall in an honorable, though lost, cause.

There is also this random thought: What ruined the *Literary Digest*'s notorious 1936 poll which showed Landon as a shoo-in was that it was taken among telephone subscribers. This one was taken among automobile owners, a notably affluent group.

We Missourians who disagree with each other on how to say the name of our state aren't really mad at the other fellow and often pray for him.

Save the. . . What Did You Call It?

"There it was. All alone. Its magnificent head lifted as though already it had scented danger. Its pelt shimmered irridescently in the effulgent rays of the setting sun.

"Moving in with my camera, I incautiously sent a pebble clinking down the gorge. In a flash, before it could be photographed, what may be the last Great Bald Weasel in the world had disappeared into the impenetrable underbrush.

"And that, gentlemen of the foundation, is why I am here. Unless something is done now, and I mean now, the Great Bald Weasel will be no more."

That is more or less the way I will open the presentation. It needs some polishing, of course. I want to check on a couple of words, such as irridescently and effulgent, but the rough outline gives, I should think, an idea of the effect I am after.

Ripples of indignation will squirm around the room.

I will be dressed the way conservationists dress, another detail I'll have to verify. Anyway, I will select a white-haired member of the board and address myself to him:

"Sir, you will remember when you were a barefoot tad, before you climbed the ladder of free enterprise to eminence in the social-cultural complex, when the Great Bald Weasel roamed the prairies in vast herds, stretching from horizon to horizon as far as the eye could see. And when their annual migratory flights darkened the sun. Now, may I ask you, sir, when is the last time you saw a Great Bald Weasel?"

His spectacles will be removed while he wipes away a tear.

"Son," he will say, "it has been years. It seems like decades. Tell you the truth, I don't know when I last saw a Great Bald Weasel."

"And you, madam," I continue, addressing a sensibly tweedy matron, "are you aware of the number of runaway children snatched from the jaws of disaster and returned to their family circles as recently as 1926, all because of the heroism of Great Bald Weasels? . . . I thought not. The public memory is short. But these papers which I brandish aloft show that not one [slowly, letting it sink in] not one child has been rescued by a Great Bald Weasel in the last fiscal year.

"My proposal is modest. If the foundation will fund the operation, including my merely adequate stipend for a year, I think we can mount a self-supporting campaign to save the Great Bald Weasel."

I do not delude myself that everything will go smoothly. These foundations are hardly anybody's fool. A thin-faced chap will rise with the predictable complaint:

"Research shows that the Great Bald Weasel does not exist."

My tactic will be one of complete candor.

"Of course it doesn't," I will say, "and that is why this campaign to save it has such unimaginable financial possibilities. You start a crusade to save the chicken and possible donors will laugh and say, 'Why, heck, I see chickens every day.' Which they can't say about the Great Bald Weasel. Instead they will think, 'By golly, that's right. I just never see Great Bald Weasels,' and reach for their checkbooks.

"Also, we can build a good public image for the Great Bald Weasel. Nobody hates it. The Save the Alligator people face a problem because there are a lot of folks who flat out don't like alligators.

"People from all walks and wallows of life will send in five dollars or more to save the Bald Weasel. Species-saving is the biggest thing in America right now, but nobody has ever cashed in on it. It's the shocking truth that not one cent was ever made off the whooping crane.

"The Save the Bald Weasel campaign, properly handled, can be bigger than General Motors."

And of course, it will all come to nothing, because foundations don't want to make money, especially dishonestly.

It's a shame too. I could use the $150,000 a year as director, plus the travel allowance. The last Great Bald Weasel was seen on the Riviera, so that would have been the first place I would have looked.

Don't Forget the Guys

This fellow was mailing a large package to some elsewhere or other and I asked him how come. He said it was potato chips he was sending to his son.

"In outermost Siberia, I presume?"

"No," he said and named a relatively civilized part of the country, if any remain.

"They don't have potato chips there?" I inquired.

"Probably," he said, "they do. But they do not have the exact brand upon which the tad has been nurtured for his entire thirty-nine years. So every week my wife buys a sack of potato chips and I mail them. I am the subject of some curiosity around the postoffice as the man who weekly mails these large, light boxes. A person who mails potato chips gets to be known."

He mailed his potato chips to the East Coast and I thought about the matter while I mailed the chocolate cookies to the West Coast. There are chocolate cookies up and down our Pacific shores. I am sure there are. And large, sanitary, well-lighted factories to produce them as well as convenient stores in which they are sold.

In fact, I imagine that if any young person were to leave California, although I have never heard of one doing so, his parents would be mailing chocolate cookies to him in Indianapolis, Cincinnati, or wherever he might land.

We are constantly assaulted upon the eardrum by people agonizing that America is homogenized, that its parts are interchangeable, that Bridgeport is Anaheim and Coos Bay is Ocala. There may be a modicum of truth in this impeachment, but if it were really accurate, why are the mails full of potato chips and chocolate cookies and peanut brittle and boysenberry jam, all passing one another in the cargo compartments of fan jets in the dark and brooding night?

I think Americans are becoming more and more attached to the products of their hometowns precisely at the time that they are becoming increasingly rootless. As a bunch of alienated Ishmaels spread over the continent you'd think we would be less attached to things back where we came from.

But we cannot bear the pang of being completely without some link to the old neighborhood. That is why we hanker after the doughnuts that only Mrs. Empathy made in her little old bakery on the corner and will awaken in foreign lands overcome by gustatory nostalgia.

The situation is parodied by the Beautiful People of whom we read, the ones who have their favorite New York bagels flown to Los Angeles or their avocadoburgers jetted to them in the opposite direction.

Texans have their chili mailed to them from home no matter where they wander, and Michiganders over the foam eagerly await a shipment of goat milk fudge from the old environs.

My rough guess is that 86.7 percent of the parcel post traffic in this country consists of delicacies being mailed to people from places where they used to live.

It takes up the slack caused by what I assume to be the decline in the mailing of laundry. There was a time when young men and women, living away from home, sent their laundry back to mother every week. The carefree young bachelor could be identified by those brown boxes made of something between cardboard and tin which they carried to the postoffice every Monday. A little window on the front contained a reversible card; one side was addressed to Mom and the other to the boy away.

I don't see them any more. I suppose the launderettes or the washeteria have made this particular arrangement irrelevant.

In the days of the laundry box, mother would lovingly tuck

some goodies in with the shirts and socks. Now the cookies and, yes, potato chips, are mailed on their own.

It's a kind of appealing picture of America, to me at any rate, that fathers in Montgomery, Alabama, are mailing dill pickles to married children in Detroit, where you can't get a decent dill pickle. Except, of course, for those that Detroit parents are sending to their offspring in Montgomery.

We will never be a nation of dull conformity as long as we don't think we are, and the mails continue to run.

❖❖❖❖

Love Message from a Cheapskate

V—is for the Vapid sentiments expressed on Valentine cards in the stores this year. Honestly I don't think they would be halfway good enough for you. It's not like the wonderful ones they used to have, like "We'd Make a Peach of a Pear" with a picture of the appropriate fruit and only cost a nickel, tops. Now it's just all sorts of sickening stuff and you're lucky if you get off for fifty cents.

A—means Automobile, which is something you really would have enjoyed for Valentine's, until you stopped and thought about it. It also stands for Almost, which is how close I came to buying you one. But I'll tell you, sweetheart, I went out to the garage and took a look at the old car and, darn it, maybe I'm an old softie, but there is a heap o' livin' in that old heap. I just couldn't bear to break your heart by trading it in, as I know it would have. After you had time to think about it.

L—stands for Let-out which you can certainly do with all those several dresses in the closet in which you have looked like a queen down through the wonderful years. Oh, sure, there are a lot of fancy gewgaws in the shops, but those wonderful old dresses are really you. I was telling Mom the other day how clever you were with a needle. She sent her regards.

E—is for Ecology and also Endangered Species, which explains why there is no fur coat this year. Could you find true happiness in a garment made from the pelts of furry friends who are not only worth perserving for their own sake but who thin out the herds of hunters by biting them in the leg? I'll tell you, dumpling, you had a narrow escape from having our relationship spoiled by a full-length beaver. It was beautiful, though, as I told the man when I sent it back, so as not to hurt his feelings.

N—stands for Nothing in the fanciest shops in town which is good enough for my baby.

T—means Taxes, a subject which is close to my heart at this time of year. You have been a loyal deduction, and I appreciate it. But I know that you would not want me to shirk my responsibility to the government, which does so much for all of us, just for new living-room draperies. Don't blame me because Valentine's is so close to April 15. Go argue with Cupid.

I—is for Internal Revenue, but I have mentioned that. Also it stands for Indigestion, which you know you always get when you eat too much candy. I had a swell box picked out for you. Five pounds, big red bow, little glassine insert telling you where all the crummy soft centers were so you could have left them for somebody else. I had it under my arm and then I wondered how I would feel if I traded the glow I would receive from giving you this candy for the possible serious illness which might ensue. You know how you stuff yourself.

N—represents Next Year when we will take that Caribbean cruise I promised you in 1953. What a great Valentine that would be. But isn't it even better to look forward to it? I have been hearing bad reports of hurricanes and things like that down around those islands, and we wouldn't want anything like that to spoil our perfect vacation, now would we? Remember, cupcake, the present comes and goes, but Next Year is forever.

E—is for Envy. I hate to say it. But some of your friends are going to turn green when they learn of all the thoughtfulness and planning I have put into making this a truly memorable Valentine's day for you. Would Ed or Sam or Marvin or any of the others have done the same?

S—stands merely for Sob, an expression of the feelings which overcome me as I read this acrostic of my love. I trust and hope, and even pray, that you will feel the same.

❖❖❖❖

Twelve Days of Flu

There are those who would have us believe that the Hong Kong flu is not among us this year with its customary virulence. Anyone who checks office absenteeism or his own temperature knows that this is not true. When a man begins to feel a little bug going around within him he checks the medicine cabinet for remedies and searches his files for something that will permit him to take a day off while at the same time sharing his experiences with similarly suffering mankind.

> On the first day of Hong Kong
> My true love gave to me
> An aspirin in a toddy.
>
> On the second day of Hong Kong
> My true love gave to me

Two decongestants and
An aspirin in a toddy.

On the third day of Hong Kong
My true love gave to me
Three chest rubs,
Two decongestants, and
An aspirin in a toddy.

On the fourth day of Hong Kong
My true love gave to me
Four chicken soups,
Three chest rubs,
Two decongestants, and
An aspirin in a toddy.

On the fifth day of Hong Kong
My true love gave to me
Five vitamins,
Four chicken soups,
Three chest rubs,
Two decongestants, and
An aspirin in a toddy.

On the sixth day of Hong Kong
My true love gave to me
Six hints at working,
Five vitamins,
Four chicken soups,
Three chest rubs,
Two decongestants, and
An aspirin in a toddy.

On the seventh day of Hong Kong
My true love gave to me
Seven digs for loafing,
Six hints at working,
Five vitamins,
Four chicken soups,
Three chest rubs,
Two decongestants, and
An aspirin in a toddy.

On the eighth day of Hong Kong
My true love gave to me
Eight bridge players cackling,
Seven digs for loafing,
Six hints at working,
Five vitamins,
Four chicken soups,
Three chest rubs,
Two decongestants, and
An aspirin in a toddy.

On the ninth day of Hong Kong
My true love gave to me
Nine bills for paying,
Eight bridge players cackling,
Seven digs for loafing,
Six hints for working,
Five vitamins,
Four chicken soups,
Three chest rubs,
Two decongestants, and
An aspirin in a toddy.

((Editor's note: And so it goes on. In the interest of brevity, we will omit the tenth and eleventh days.)

On the twelfth day of Hong Kong
My true love gave to me
Twelve hours to get up,
Eleven looks of hatred,
Ten Cub Scouts a-yelling,
Nine bills for paying,
Eight bridge players cackling,
Seven digs for loafing,
Six hints for working,
Five smart remarks,
Four burned toasts,
Three rude snubs,
Two ultimatums, and
No whisky in the toddy.

Have You Heard the One. . .?

On a peak in the high Himalayas two weary mountain climbers approached the hut of a Sherpa tribesman. Night was coming and the menacing clouds indicated that a storm was about to break.

In front of the hut sat an old man playing tribal melodies upon a nose flute. The mountain climbers asked if they might spend the night in his hut. He assented and offered to share his humble repast.

"My wife," he said, "will rustle up some grub."

After thanking him the mountain climbers entered the hut.

There they saw their host's wife being embraced by an abominable snowman.

One of the climbers rushed outside and cried to the old man, "Say, do you know there is an abominable snowman kissing your wife?"

"No," the tribesman replied, "but hum a few bars and I'll fake it."

This is a joke which, except for the last line, I have just thought up.

Several readers have indicated that I do not offer enough boons to mankind, but this, they will have to agree, is a boon unequaled. It is the all-purpose, unstoppable joke. The trouble with most of us (or with me, anyway) is that we never get a chance to tell our jokes.

We start out and say, "Stop me if you have heard this one," and somebody stops us. There is no joke that somebody in the crowd hasn't heard before—and most jokes give themselves away in the first few lines.

The man who is frustrated by being stopped in mid-joke is an unhappy man, and unhappiness leads to all sorts of marital discord and kitchen drinking.

Go back and reread this joke. You have, of course, heard it before. Everybody has heard it. You have heard the punch line, that is. You have not heard the part about the mountain climbers and the tribesman and the nose flute and the abominable snowman.

I heard it at least fifteen years ago and the way it was then was that a fellow came down from the apartment above to complain about a man playing the piano too loudly at three o'clock in the morning.

"Do you know there is a little old lady sick upstairs?" he demanded angrily.

"No," replied the piano player, "but hum a few bars and I'll fake it."

Since then I have heard at least five variations. Each time I was completely suckered in, as was everybody else in the group. We went right along, letting the man tell his joke until he came to the punch line, and by that time it wasn't worth stopping him.

With this one joke, I firmly believe, a man can build up a reputation as a raconteur that will make him a legend in his own time.

Have you heard the one about the President going to Nepal to ask the Dahlia Lama advice on the latest world crisis? Of course you haven't. It goes like this:

The President decided that he should seek the advice of the wisest men in the world about the crisis. In order not to alert the press he made secret pilgrimages to philosophers and scientists, theologians and military strategists in all parts of America and Europe. They were all helpful, but still the answer eluded him.

His course was clear. He must go to Asia to get the thinking of the greatest brain of our age.

It was not an easy trip. Parties of engineers had to be sent ahead (in secrecy) to hew from the brooding mountainside a landing strip that could accommodate the presidential jet.

Finally, the president arrived. By jeep he made the last few painful miles from the landing strip to the monastery where he found the Dahlia Lama sonorously chanting.

"Sir," he said, breathlessly, "I don't have much time. I have come many long, weary miles to talk with you. Do you know Saudi Arabia is about to fall into Russia's hands like a ripe apple?"

"No," said the Lama calmly, "but hum a few bars and I'll fake it."

Do you see how simple it is? With this joke I guarantee that no one will stop you until you have finished. After you have finished, of course, you're on your own.

Our Washington Correspondent

Aunt Fern Pottle, retired editor for forty-two years of the "Items from Isosceles" column in the Oblong, Oklahoma, Weekly Oboe, sends us "Newsy News from Our Nation's Capital." We have been concerned about her and were relieved to receive this report from Washington, where Aunt Fern makes her home with her daughter, Mrs. Zoe (Bun) Tump and her son-in-law, Jim Tom Tump.

Friends of Mrs. Fern Pottle from roundabout the Oblong and Isosceles areas will be interested to know that Mrs. Pottle did not meet Princess Anne and Prince Charles Windsor, who have been visitors in Our Nation's Capital from elsewhere.

From what could be judged at a distance, the young people from Overseas, where their parents are with the government, seemed to be quite nice. Although his hair was somewhat longer than is the style at Kigowah County Consolidated High School he is in no sense a "zoot-suiter" of the type so often encounted that it makes one wonder about the parents of today.

The other ladies of the quill reported that Princess Anne didn't seem to be having a good time. Mrs. Fern Pottle can't say for sure as she was not invited to any of the Social Events and wouldn't have gone anyway as she is busy looking after her daughter, Zoe (Bun) Tump, and her son-in-law, Jim Tom Tump, as well as their two lovely children, Sean and Vikki.

If Mrs. Pottle had been asked, which she wasn't, she would have been glad to entertain the Princess, as she has always gotten along well with "young folks" and often hears from those who attended her Sunday school class which she taught for thirty-five years. Not one of them is a "lounge lizard," "flapper," or "jelly bean."

Mrs. Pottle would have had a covered dish supper, with

card games such as Snap and Fish and the exchanging of ten-cent Mystery Gifts. She bets the Princess would have had plenty to talk about when she got back to the Old Country.

The Princess missed out on meeting Zoe (Bun) Tump, neé Pottle, who not only looks quite a bit like her (only more mature) but has the coincidence of being "royalty" herself, having been Chemical Fertilizer Queen of the Kigowah County Fair in 1957, as many will remember. They could have had a good Hah! Hah! over that.

Farm folk will be interested to know that we have had good local rains in the Washington area this summer. Mrs. Pottle wishes she could send some of it back to the country around Oblong, where, she sees by the *Oboe*, there is considerable blowing dust.

The First Family have left their lovely house here, one of the nicest in town, for a visit home. Washington is a fascinating city, being Our Nation's Capital, but many here retain an affection for their Old Home Place, like the First Family, who could go to a different Social Event of some kind almost every day if they wanted to, but often slip away to greet old friends and make new ones.

Mrs. Fern Pottle understands. Even though she has a lovely home here with her son-in-law, Jim Tom Tump, who has just received a sideways promotion in auto parts, she often thinks of the dear faces in Oklahoma and continues to take the *Oblong Oboe* (The Old Reliable) which she reads from cover to cover although some of the names are strange now and others have gone.

And she wishes she could slip away like the First Family to wander among the old, familiar haunts "where the woodbine twineth." But airline tickets cost the world and Jim Tom Tump says, "Mom, we just can't afford it right now."

God bless all at home.

MARCH

Song of the Shoveler

For the really enthusiastic snowshoveler, a late winter snowfall is a happy dividend. It is what Indian summer is to the golfer—one last chance to enjoy a favorite pastime before the season ends. It is a sort of lagniappe, although it doesn't snow very much in the parts of this country where lagniappe is a common word.

A devotee of the shovel writes rather poetically of his feelings in the matter:

"When I have suffered through a week or so of mild days and am just about resigned to putting the old shovel up on the rafters of the garage for another summer, you can imagine the thrill of delight with which I hear the cheery voice of my good wife calling to me that it has snowed during the night.

"I spring to the window, and sure enough there is all that beautiful white stuff waiting to be shoveled. The game is afoot. Impatiently I hurry through breakfast, then don my mackinaw, heaviest trousers, tippet and boots.

"My hands curve themselves naturally around my trusty old shovel. What good times we have known. Sometimes my good wife swears I care more about that old shovel than I do her. Well, maybe that's going it a bit strong. But there's no doubt that a man and his shovel do establish a rapport, they work easily together.

"Maybe you have noticed that a man tends to resemble the equipment of whatever hobby or sport excites him most. Thus, the hunter will look like his hound, the bowler will tend to resemble a bowling ball, the fisherman a worm, and the golfer a niblick or perhaps a mashie.

"My wife says she swears that I look more like my snow shovel every year. And while I laugh it off I must admit there is a resemblance, especially in profile.

"Now I know that more and more women are taking up snow-shoveling and I am glad to see it. There is plenty of snow for all, I tell them, and certainly a lady who is shoveling snow is mighty attractive, what can be seen of her anyway.

"Still, the real mystique of snow-shoveling, the spiritual inwardness so to speak, is, I think, beyond the feminine grasp. No criticism of the ladies, bless them.

"But a man alone out in the cold, deserted street with his snow shovel, maybe a curl of smoke from his trusty pipe curling around his head, there is a man who feels at ease with Nature and himself.

"He sort of thinks he is cheated if the snow season is a short one. Some years it appears to be over before a man really gets his backswing and his follow through and his hip action all coordinated and remembers to keep his left knee locked and all the other little details.

"'Poetry in motion' is the way I have heard many an old snow-shoveler describe the perfect form of some of the great masters. Snow-shoveling keeps a man humble, too. He may think he is in top form and kid himself that he finally has the technique down pat, but then he will pull off a really horrendous swing, covering himself with snow, tossing a poorly aimed shot through the back door or something like that.

50

And isn't it always the way, that this happens when people are watching? But the veteran snow-shoveler just laughs and knows there will be another day.

"So that's why it is wonderful to get a good snow along in March or April. It's a whole new chance to work at improving one's game, which is a lifetime assignment.

"Still there's something sad about it. You know that there won't be many more snows if any this year and there will be the long summer of reading books of instructions by some of the giants of shoveling or maybe oiling the shovel or at least patting its handle.

"Wouldn't it be great if the television networks would send men to the South Pole to photograph shoveling there so we could watch it on television in our home this summer?

"Even if they put it on closed circuit and charged ten dollars a ticket, a lot of real hard core snow shovelers would be happy to pay."

❖❖❖❖

The Wearin' o' the Leek

We Welsh always wear a leek in our hat on St. David's Day, and don't ask me when St. David's Day is, because we Welsh are a dour, uncommunicative lot except when singing in an eisteddfod or originating names of towns that are so long that Mr. Robert Ripley wrote them up in "Believe It or Not."

The main thing I like about us Welsh is that we don't try to get everybody else into the act.

On St. David's Day we don't hit other people on the back and say, "Hey, Mac, I don't see no leek in your hat. You anti-Welsh or something?"

We spare you the legendary feats of Madog ap Maredudd

51

and Rhys ap Gruffyd, perhaps because, until we had looked in the *Encyclopaedia Britannica*, we had never heard of them.

We do not fill the airwaves with songs about Welsh eyes, Welsh sweethearts, or work-ravaged Welsh mothers. We take it calmly.

In Britain, only Wales has the lesser whitebeam, the rock cinauefoil, yellow whitlow grass, Cotoneaster, mountain spiderwort, and the grass Mibora minima. But do we hire tenors to bellow the virtues of these lovely flowers, the way the Irish do about shamrocks and roses, neither of which, incidentally, is exclusively Irish? You know we don't.

Although it is well known that the Welsh are the world's greatest singers, you can go into a restaurant, tavern, or hotel lobby on St. David's Day without hearing a peep out of us. The Irish, on the other hand—but let's not belabor the obvious.

If pressed, of course, I could do you a splendid job on "The March of the Men of Harlech," but I do not volunteer it the way others assault complete strangers with the news that Ireland must be heaven because their mither came from there.

I love the Irish. Everybody loves the Irish.

Nobody loves the Welshmen. We go our lonely way, a dark, taciturn, moody people. We do not need affection, or green beer, or shamrock-shaped pizzas. We do not need to remind ourselves once a year that we are better than other people, we Welsh. We are not even sure that we are.

You cannot make a career out of being a Welshman. There has not been a professional Welshman since Owen Glendower.

We are not jealous of all the fuss that is made over the Irish on St. Patrick's Day, with a green line down the middle of Fifth Avenue and all the rest of it.

But there is one nagging thought. I heard an airline flies

over shamrocks from Ireland every March 17 and distributes them. It seems odd that with all us Welsh (there must be as many Joneses as there are Kellys) they couldn't fly over some leeks for us to put in our hats on St. David's Day—whenever that is and whatever a leek is.

Not, of course, that we proud, solitary folk would ever ask a favor. . . .

❖❖❖❖❖

The Umbrella

Friends, I know that there are worse problems in the world. I read the papers. But it's hard to concentrate on the big worries when you have a small one going for you at the same time.

The thing that happens is that you carry an umbrella to work on a rainy morning and when you leave that afternoon the weather has cleared and you walk off and forget the umbrella.

The next day your wife says, threateningly, "Don't forget the umbrella, Sam."

It is a bright day, full of sunshine. That afternoon you have the problem of carrying the umbrella home on the bus without looking like some species of filbert.

Bus stop humorists are unable to resist the sight of a man carrying an umbrella when the nearest rain cloud is hovering over Intermittent, North Dakota.

"Well, Mr. Chamberlain," they will say, "does it look like peace in our time?"

If it's a raincoat you are involved with you can wrap it up and stick it in a paper sack or some such. But how are you going to wrap an umbrella so it looks like anything but an umbrella?

You can, of course, sit as far away from the umbrella as you can and pretend that it doesn't belong to you. But this can be tricky.

I tried it one time and an acquaintance sat down next to me and said, "Is that your umbrella?"

"Why, uh, no," I said. "I just found it."

And he said, "Oh," rather suspiciously, so when I got to the stop near my house I had to take the umbrella and, because the acquaintance was watching me (a fellow I never really liked), I had to turn it in to the bus driver and tell him that I seemed to have found this umbrella.

Then, the next morning, I had to call the lost-and-found department of the bus company and ask them if anybody had found my umbrella.

"No, sir," the man said after he had gone away from the phone for a while to see about it. "We got a left shoe and a trombone but no umbrella."

"I happen to know better," I said. "My umbrella was found yesterday on bus No. 18975 and turned in to the driver."

"How come you're so sure?"

"Because I found it myself."

Click!

A half hour later I had my wife call and by this time they had found the umbrella and asked her to describe it, which she did.

"When did you say your husband lost the umbrella?" the man asked her.

"Yesterday."

"What was your husband doing carrying an umbrella yesterday?" the man wanted to know. "The sun shone all day."

"Because he is a nut," said my wife.

"Is he the same one who called a while ago and said he found his own umbrella and gave it to the driver?"

"I'm afraid so," said my wife.

"You poor thing," said the man.

I finally got the umbrella back. But not that day because it was raining too hard to go to the lost-and-found place. I had to wait until the next day, when the sun was shining.

I got it home by running it down one leg of my pants, with the handle hooked over my belt. There were only a few people on the bus but I had to stand up all the way home because of the umbrella in my pants leg.

The same acquaintance got on and asked why I didn't sit down next to him and I told him, "No, sir, I got in enough trouble sitting next to you a couple of days ago."

He went and sat behind the driver, and when I got off I'm pretty sure I heard one of them say to the other, "That nut looks like he's got an umbrella in there somewhere."

❖❖❖❖

The Listener's Bureau

There was a time when I made speeches after dinners and after luncheons. I am neither bragging nor apologizing, although I do feel a little embarrassed about one or two I made after breakfasts, which does seem a bit early in the day.

Now I have switched to the other side of the lectern; but my attitude is much the same. I used to think that a speaker should be paid for his efforts. Now my position is that it is the listener who should have the honorarium forced upon him.

From my new viewpoint it seems ridiculous that the speaker should be getting the money while the listener actually pays out of his own pocket.

Look at the average confrontation between speaker and audience. Who is having the fun? Obviously the speaker. He has had the free run of the hospitality room before the ceremonies began, he is telling about his own early life, his struggle for success, his guideposts for significant living, all the stuff he couldn't get his own mother, much less wife, to listen to under normal circumstances. At the head table the food was served first and he has forked his last bit of apricot cobbler while the audience is still struggling with the Waldorf salad.

And he is getting paid.

The peasantry in the pit have paid $7.50 or worse, plus whatever they laid out at the cash bar, the $1.50 to park the car and all the extras. As a reward what they get to do is listen. Nobody wants to listen.

Leading psychologists agree and experience demonstrates that listening is a much more difficult job than talking. Everybody wants to talk; nobody wants to listen.

So what weird logic is it that says the talker should be paid and the listener should pay?

I am calling for a revolution in this matter. I am working on the details, but my approach is that I (or you or anybody else) would charge a basic $50 fee for listening to any speech. It isn't much, I know, but we have to start small in order to build a reputation. Volume is a factor. In a week a man could easily listen to four speeches. At $50 apiece plus travel expenses it would certainly be a nice bit of extra income.

When I complete my prospectus I think it will call for five dollars for listening to each joke told by the speaker. If it is a joke that the speaker pretends to have been reminded of by the company here tonight (e.g. a doctor joke at a medical meeting) the price goes to ten dollars.

Childhood reminiscences by the speaker call for an additional payment of $15 a listening minute. Explanations of why he is glad to be here this evening and mention of relatives living in the neighborhood are another $25. Any reference to his wife as The Better Half, Little Woman, or My Bride will draw an automatic $37.50 surcharge.

When asked to listen to a speech I will inquire how long a speech they want listened to. At twenty minutes I start a meter running. It could get pretty expensive.

Someone will ask where the money is to come from if all the speech-listeners are paid. Obviously from the speaker. As I have said he is getting all these beautiful side benefits of basking in the spotlight and spouting his opinions. Instead of receiving $1,500 let him put up that amount.

There are now speakers' bureaus which advertise authors and countesses and congressmen and explorers who will speak for a fee. How about a listeners' bureau, giving the names of those of us who will travel the length and breadth of the land to hear speeches, for the proper pecuniary compensation?

The point is made that this plan is economically unsound; that if it were put into effect nobody would make after-dinner speeches.

Justice is justice; fair is fair, and if that's what happens we'll just have to live with it.

❖❖❖❖

On Sharing

A sports-writing friend brought up a semi-demi-thought the other day which I can't quite put out of my mind. At the same time, I don't know exactly what to do about it.

He said, apropos of an interview he had just had, that he was puzzled by what a coach means when he says, "We will win our share of games."

"I mean, you know," he said (sportswriters talk that way), "what is his team's share? Who decides it?"

As I say, I tried to ignore the problem or refuse to admit that the problem existed.

But it has been nagging at me like a rough place on a tooth, and I have been bringing the massive brain to bear upon it. First of all, it should be said that I have read many and many a story about how the Skipper predicts that his team will win its share, without questioning exactly what he meant by it. I accepted it as one of those empty phrases which we can't get too many of in these troubled times because they have a cheerful sound to them.

Pursuing the matter, I realized that I have never heard of a coach after winning, let us say, four games, calling a press conference to announce:

"Well, boys, that's it. We've won our share. No need to be greedy. Fair's fair. From now on we're going to lose."

It doesn't happen. As far as I know.

You would think that if a football team has a season in which it posts one victory against ten defeats, the wily mentor would summon the media to report that all had gone according to his plan.

"As I told you back in September," he could say, clambering up on a chair so those in the back could hear, "we would win our share this year. Our share was one game. We won it. Thank you very much."

But coaches don't seem to do that. I wonder why?

Can it be that they don't know what their share is?

Of course, we may extend our examination of this problem beyond the narrow sphere of sports.

How often do we hear a man, full of years and honors, reminiscing about his life and saying, "I made my share of mistakes."

And we nod and say, "Yes, yes" or "Not at all" or "Hum." Something on that order. What we should do is question this man closely. He has important information. Exactly how many mistakes has he made? How can he be sure they were his share? He could easily have a few more mistakes coming to him.

If I make more than my share of mistakes does this cut down on somebody else's share?

"I have had my share of troubles," someone will tell you. What?

This is getting rather metaphysical. Is the implication that there are a finite number of troubles in the world and we are all entitled to just so many and no more? What if you get your share of mistakes and troubles out of the way by the time you are twenty-one? Does this mean you are home free for the rest of your life? Or does whoever is in charge issue you another share?

People not only speak of their share of trouble but of their share of happiness. All the same questions arise.

Frankly, I wish these sportwriters would confine themselves to just giving the scores and quoting the coaches without bothering themselves or me by what anything means.

I don't need something else to worry about.

I've got my share.

❖❖❖❖

A Star Is Born

I have found a way to attract attention at any social gathering, something I had always found difficult in the past, being of a rather mousy, nondescript appearance with the kind of personality that makes me indistinguishable from the wallpaper, except that the wallpaper is more exciting.

Now I find I am lionized wherever I go. And the best part is that you can't do the same thing, because for you it is too late.

I don't know my astrological sign.

It's as simple as that. Lovely ladies cluster around, screaming out: "Hey, Madge, here's one who doesn't know whether he's a Scorpio or a Libra."

They want my autograph. They honestly do. They have never encountered anybody before who didn't know what sign he was born under. I do know the date on which I was born, but I don't tell anybody because I'm afraid that if I did they would tell me I was a Virgo or a Taurus or one of those things, and I don't want to know.

What I lose in birthday presents I pick up in prestige.

As I say, it's too late for you, because you know all about your horoscope and don't pretend that you don't. I know all about you. You think you can impress people by opening a conversation with the information that you had been born on the cusp of Aquarius or some such. You think you can initiate interesting conversations that way.

Perhaps you can. But, believe me, it's nothing to compare with not knowing your sign.

If there was ever a subject where ignorance outdraws knowledge any day, it's astrology.

People, particularly women, admire a man who has the courage to face life without the least idea of what the cosmic configurations are conspiring for him. There is a bit of dash here.

It is flying in the face of fate almost as daringly as not knowing your blood type or the night number of your insurance agent.

It is not easy to keep one's astrological innocence pristine. A man tends to have a family, members of which know when he was born. They will make insinuations that he is a Pisces or worse, and try such ruses as handing him a paper napkin with the appropriate sign printed upon it.

I never accept paper napkins unless they say something forthright, such as "Drink Noodnick's Beer." A man learns to sense these things. If he gets the idea that he is about to be apprised of his horoscope, he flees the room with his hands over his ears.

Sorry as his plight was, a certain romantic aura surrounded The Man Without a Country. The same applies to The Man Without an Astrological Sign.

He is marked wherever he goes. Whispers follow him.

There are advantages other than status, of course. Not knowing what stars were where when one was born confers a great freedom of action. A man can take trips when he wants, launch business enterprises as the mood strikes, and be cautious about personal relationships if that is the way he feels about it. No worries about what the stars say.

He doesn't even have to mutter, "Of course, I don't believe in this stuff, but—" as he scans the predictions for that day.

Astrology fans should not be angry or disappointed that I feel this way. I am not knocking the belief of the believers.

I am not speaking for disbelief but rather for ignorance. I find that having no idea of my proper place in the cosmos frees me of a great deal of time-consuming worry.

It also, as I have said, gets me invited out a lot. What a feather in the cap of any hostess to have among her guests the only man in town who doesn't know whether he is a Leo or a Crab.

❖❖❖❖

Cat Man

There was a picture of me the other day in the paper holding a cat. I was holding a cat, the paper wasn't; I have always had trouble with sentence structure.

People have said to me, particularly people who know me well, who number three, that they hadn't thought I was a cat person. I'm not sure what that means, and whether it is an insult or a compliment. Some of the people I admire the most, like T. S. Eliot and Edward Lear, were cat lovers. But there is

61

a kind of miasma of old-maidishness connected with a man who likes cats.

Students of the photograph may have noticed that I was gripping the subject cat firmly (but gently) around the throat to keep it from either escaping or shredding my shirt, which is one of its favorite pastimes, now that we have run out of destroyable furniture.

Now I am not taking this early spring day to get into any sort of argument about cats or whatever.

What I want to point out is that the fact you have a cat on the premises does not mean you are a cat person.

What you will discover, young readers, is that as you grow older you end up with the household pets that your children have gone away and left you with. They may or may not be the ones of your choice.

It's sort of like the man whose taste in clothes is commented on. The thing is that his wife or some other near and dear has color coordinated him and he is only wearing what he has been told to put on.

A picture of me taken at any other time might have shown me as a dog man, coonhound, whippet, English bulldog, a long and varied string. And people would have said, "He doesn't look like a coonhound man or a bulldog man." And I wasn't, although I liked them both well enough. After all, you get along with what you have, whether it is alive or a ghastly clock inherited from Aunt Bella.

There were periods when if the photographer wanted to add a touch of domesticity he could have portrayed me with 345 white mice, or with six snakes (which is where the white mice went).

It would not have been fair to call me a mouse man or a snake man. Then there was the turtle period, the alligator episode, the guinea pigs, and the chinchilla.

(Folks, you should have been there the morning that the guinea pig ate the chinchilla, or the other way around.)

The thing I want to impress upon you is not to judge a man by whatever beasties run about his home. He may not be responsible for them at all. A child gets married. The furniture goes, the best pictures go. The little creatures remain at home to keep the old folks from rattling around in the big house.

So when you see a picture of a man of mature years with a cat, don't assume that he is an ailurophile. Nor does it mean that he doesn't like cats. It just means that he's making the best of what he has and is thankful it's not a horse.

❖❖❖❖

Pity the Poor Rich

As far as I am concerned the argument over whether it is better to be rich or poor never got off the ground. The former, it has always seemed to me, was the clear winner.

And yet, while I am a long way from celebrating the virtues of poverty, I do think that something may be said for a certain decent indigence.

I was started on this line of thought by a friend who told me that he and his wife had received a letter from wealthy friends who had purchased an elaborate camper, or recreational vehicle as I believe they are called, and subjected themselves to a long and miserable trip.

My friend's wife's comment was: "If they hadn't been rich they wouldn't have had to do it."

True, true.

When one reads about the doings of the well-to-do who have thrust themselves into costumes to toodle around to a gala ball, dripping with Balinese decor or worse, one tends to view the undershirt, the can of beer, the well-thumbed Thucydides, and the company of a few old friends as infinitely preferable. The rich man (or his wife at any rate) must be under constant pressure to attend social events which sound, at least to the casual reader, both cruel and unusual.

They must spend a working man's annual stipend merely to go to some foreign spa so that they can complain about its deterioration.

Marriage counselors tell us that many a little family flounders on the rock of financial difficulties. Yes, but I'm not sure but what a little reasonable poverty helps keep things going.

Another friend once told me that there was a time when his wife would have left him but she couldn't afford to hire a sitter to stay with the children while she went downtown to see a lawyer.

Most of us can leaf through even the flossiest magazines and study the ads without the slightest tremor of the hand. The diamonds, the furs, the $2,500 wristwatches do not tempt us. They are remote as the mountains and other topographical features of the moon. We can admire their beauty and pass on.

But I suppose there comes a level of income where these things enter the realm of possibility and a certain clamminess evidences itself.

To put it in even homelier terms, all reasonable persons agree that the best food in the world is leftovers. Still I am given to understand that the rich do not eat leftovers, unless they have been given a French name and served up, flaming, amid the subdued lights and silken draperies of a posh eatery.

Is it worth it to be rich beyond the dreams of avarice if it means giving up leftovers?

Probably yes.

But it is something to consider.

When the late Riley spoke of going back "to Grigsby's station where we wuz so happy and so pore" he probably overstated the case. He who sings the joys of poverty can easily make that mistake.

I am merely making a few observations which may bring some comfort to the man who is lying in his middle-income hammock and pondering the plight of the wealthy. Especially since there probably is not very much he can, or intends to, do about it.

❖❖❖❖

Inexcusable

A late, lamented friend, whenever he wanted to slip out of the office for whatever purpose, would announce that he was going to step up to the corner newsstand to see if the new *Collier's* had come in.

He used this excuse for many years after the demise of *Collier's*.

I don't know that it would work today, even if he changed the name of the magazine, because there really isn't anything on the periodical racks that a man might reasonably rush out to buy.

We all remember Uncle Ed who would tell Aunt Zoe every evening that he was going down to the cellar to bank the furnace for the night. This enabled him to have a restorative nip. The thermostat and other refinements now take care of the furnace or at least have eliminated it as an excuse.

So many of the old alibis have gone, and the question arises whether we are developing new ones to take their place.

There was a time when you could explain tardiness at school by saying that the buckle on your knickerbockers was broken. Now, I suppose, you could tell the teacher that you couldn't find a place to park.

In the old days when the collar button was ubiquitous you told Mr. Frobisher that you were late to work because your collar button rolled under the bureau and it took you fifteen minutes to find it. Now the collar button has vanished. Or anyway there is no reason to look for it. It may still be under the bureau. In any event it is finished as an excuse for anything.

That is no reason for giving up and admitting that you overslept.

"Why," you can tell Mr. Frobisher, "I would have been here an hour ago but the battery in my electric toothbrush was dead and I had to wait for the stores to open so I could buy a replacement."

"It could happen to anyone," he will say with a smile. "You are a fine young man and will soon receive a little something extra in your pay packet."

I suppose we must assume that every age has produced excuses that were suitable to the times. When the first caveman went to the first job he probably said he was sorry but he was delayed by being hit on the head by a pterodatyl egg. In ancient Rome it would be that a wheel came off the 8:22 chariot.

In the predictable future you can say that you checked the air pollution level before leaving home but couldn't find where the puppy had hidden your gas mask until you had hunted all over for it.

We are threatened with the age of unisex clothing, which will have one side benefit. A man can tell the boss that his wife went off in his last clean pantyhose.

Come to think of it, though, we may have a Golden Age right now. There really isn't any need for going through a lot of excuses for being late because there is hardly any way to avoid it. With traffic being what it is and the commuter trains a sometime thing, nobody is really expected to be on time.

You just walk on the job and say, "Boy, that traffic is fierce out there today."

Everybody will understand.

And if you want to slip away for a while there is no need to invent something about magazines or furnaces; you merely say you are going out to demonstrate against something.

A *Taxing Situation*

Early April is when I absent myself from felicity to tell my story to the Internal Revenue Service. Which, I hasten to assure everybody, I don't mind doing. After all, we have to buy all that vomit gas and dams and paper clips, don't we?

But what frightens me, and at the same time makes me feel that I should be memorialized in some way, is that I seem to be alone.

When someone notices my general seedy appearance in April and I explain that it is because of the, you know, income tax, they don't even know what I am talking about.

"Why," they will say, "I have this wonderful little tax man and he works it all out and gives me the result in a leather folder with my gold-leaf initials on the front."

Nobody has a big tax man. It's always "my little tax man." Word about them doesn't help me at all. It even makes me have dreams about little tax men, all in green with peaked caps. I wish I had one. (A little tax man, not a peaked cap.)

If I say to some such friends, "But I don't have a little tax man," they say, "You don't need one. Just read the instructions."

I read the instructions. I don't see any place where it says you don't have to sit around drinking black coffee, stubbing out cigarettes, yelling at your children, and kicking wastebaskets. Maybe they get different instructions than I do. All it ever says in the instructions I get is "Send the money."

Other people did their income tax returns months ago. In January. Can you imagine anybody doing a tax return in January? Apparently you can because that's when so many of you do your tax return.

I wait until April because I keep hoping that at least the weather will be better. I mean, when you're sitting there biting pencils it's nice to look out and see that there is sunshine and an occasional crocus.

All this, of course, make me a terrible anachronism, which is why I think some foundation should support me as a bit of vanishing Americana.

Especially since, as I understand it, foundation grants are nontaxable.

❖❖❖❖

April 15

Suppose you are an average American citizen—like the guy next door. Basically, your income is derived from a muck bean plantation, but you are also employed as a part-time race handicapper. Your youngest child is over seventy-two and going to college. The fourth floor of your house, which has been severely damaged by a falling meteorite, is rented out to the government for the use of the Green Berets as a training camp.

The manager of the local baseball team is dependent upon you as his sole support. One of your oil wells has started pumping orange juice. Your great-aunt, a veteran of the First

World War, has left the bulk of her fortune to your cat, which has only three legs.

Well, congratulations there, friend.

You are the one that the advice about How to Save Money on Your Income Tax is written for.

Especially if a great deal of your back pay has been impounded because you were held for a while in a Russian prison on an espionage charge and your gifts of artworks to a nonprofit institution exceeded 17 percent of your gross income.

If, of course, you are depending upon the birds to thin out your surplus cherry crop next summer, you will be interested in the deductions you can claim—the earlier the better—on the crumbs you put out for your feathered co-workers during the winter.

If you are claiming a Stutz Bearcat as an antique, while all the time you are using it as a business car, several interesting points of tax law arise.

The heartening thing is that pamphlets from the drugstore racks, columns in the daily press, half-hour interviews on the teevy answer all these questions, to say nothing of hundreds of others which closely affect the ordinary, run-of-the-mill taxpayer.

If a seven-ton monster of the horrendous deep is washed ashore in front of your beach house, can you claim it as a deduction due to the fact that its odor kept the mailman from delivering the news that you had won the Irish sweepstakes? Must you declare as income the money you received from selling balloons and little plastic souvenir monsters? If so, is this a capital gain, and may it be prorated over the approximately 350 years which is believed to be the life-span of horrendous deep-type monsters?

We ordinary people are, of course, appreciative of this advice. We don't know how we would get along without it.

But I can't help wondering if something couldn't be done

for folks who don't fit the pattern. After all, the oddball, the man who might have special problems, pays taxes, too.

Just for example, to let our imaginations run completely wild, suppose you had a man who worked for a salary and had a home and a wife and a couple of children and a year-old car and didn't own any polo ponies or spend half the year in Puerto Rico.

I will concede that a man like this has to be a figment of our imagination. He doesn't exist.

But, merely as an exercise in ingenuity, would one of the tax experts suggest some way he could keep from going either (a) broke, or (b) to Leavenworth?

It would be, I humbly submit, entertaining. I realize, of course, that it would be diverting the tax expert from more pressing matters of interest to a wider audience, such as whether a professional shot-putter, who practices in his apartment, can deduct damage to the ceiling plaster of the people downstairs as a legitimate business expense.

❖❖❖❖

A History of the Umbrella
Or
King Tut Was All Wet

It was my intention, while waiting for the rain to stop, to write a brief history of the umbrella, which is difficult to do if you don't know anything about the history of the umbrella.

Mess around in the dictionary and you will be rewarded, for your pains, with the information that its root word goes back to the same thing that inspires umbrage, both of them being involved in one of those linguistic snarls relating to some old folk language's idea of shade or shelter.

When a man takes umbrage it may mean that he has left

with your umbrella, which entitles you to take even more umbrage. None of this is to be confused with leaving in a dudgeon (an early-day two-wheeled cart).

At the moment I cannot tell you when the umbrella was invented, and please don't let me know. As far as I can tell the umbrella (or brolly) is issued to the British citizen at birth, undoubtedly paid for by the National Health Plan.

When Anglophilia was at its height in this country wealthy young Americans used to be sent by their parents to England to learn the proper way to furl, unfurl, and generally manipulate a brolly. Young people today seem to have other things on their minds.

I suppose I should explain at this point that I am writing these historical notes on paper napkins because I am trapped in this place where they don't allow minors and am unable to get to my research files because of the terrible downpour. There is only a dictionary here for settling bets.

If I had my files I could probably make this Short History quite a bit more accurate. But in the New Journalism it is not objectivity which counts, but involvement. I am involved in umbrellas at the moment. Or rather in the lack of them, or even one. My umbrella is over alongside my desk, close to my research files.

So we're just going to have to take quite a bit on faith. One of the real villains of the umbrella was Cosmo Nink, who developed the little catch which pinches the finger whenever you try to put an umbrella up or down.

Perhaps villain is too strong a word. Cosmo Nink tried to develop a release mechanism that wouldn't pinch the fingers, but he never succeeded and finally gave it up as a bad job. This is why in only moderate rains you will often see people walking around with their umbrella furled. They do not want to develop what has become known as Nink's finger. Better to get wet.

When I was a boy, men driving horse-drawn wagons used

to sit under large bicolored umbrellas. These later developed into golf, beach, and patio umbrellas, leading in turn to the invention of golf, beaches, and patios. Whether any of these were a good idea is a matter of conjecture.

Another thing you don't see any more is the parasol. The parasol kept the sol off, just as the parapluie kept off the pluie. Scholars of French will grasp my meaning.

Ladies of refinement used to carry parasols to shield them from the rays of the sun, which were thought to be harmful. This, of course, was before suntanning became a major industry.

As I have said we may not know exactly when the umbrella was invented. But we can be reasonably sure that it was introduced about two weeks before the lost, stolen, or borrowed umbrella surfaced as a staple article of humor.

Archaeologists have pointed out that many ancient tombs do not contain umbrellas. This has given rise to two schools of opinion, one holding that the umbrella had not been invented at the time of the demise of the ancient tomb's occupant, while the opposing theory is that the umbrella had been invented but had been borrowed by a friend.

Those who wish to do more research into the lore of the umbrella (or, more accurately, bumbershoot) are free to do so, as long as they don't write me about it.

At the moment the rain seems to have stopped and that's all from here.

❖❖❖❖

The 1990 Models. . .

A great deal of attention is being paid to the question of what the automobile industry ought to do to make the product safer. Maybe we're approaching this thing from the wrong end. After all, there are only a certain number of things you can do with a motorcar, the basic design of which is established by some sort of immutable natural law.

But what about people? It seems pretty obvious that we are badly designed for the motor age. Like the head up on top of the neck, which is just asking for a whiplash injury.

If the neck were eliminated, as it has been in the case of some wrestlers, it would be a major step toward traffic safety. As it is, the head bobbles around, and if it isn't being snapped backwards it's going forward and cracking the dashboard. Maybe we ought to go beyond eliminating the neck and sink the head down inside the chest where it would be protected.

Now there are those who will say "Hold on there," and "Just a minute." They will say that the design of the human body is just as much a part of the divine plan as that of the automobile.

And yet we seem to be incessantly reading about how some scientist is unlocking the key to life, unfolding the mystery of the genes, cloning, and, in general, getting ready to do humanity over.

To assume that the human body cannot be rejiggered in the noble cause of accident prevention is to be out of sync with the current thinking that man can do just about anything he programs his computers to do.

Now, of course, these changes can't be made overnight, but it doesn't look as though any major alteration in the safety design of automobiles is going to come like a bolt of lightning either.

If it is to be a long-range program, then it is not too soon to start making long-range plans. Take the matter of arms. Is two the right number? You may say yes, because that is the number we have traditionally had. But if a driver is going to steer, light a cigarette, dial the radio, hold a road map, rap the noisy child on the head, all the while waving one hand outside the car as so many motorists seem to find it necessary to do, four or five arms would seem more efficient.

Here is a good juncture at which to point out that difficult decisions will have to be made. The Conference on Redesigning the People of the United States (CORPUS) will have to approach these questions with a great deal of thoughtfulness.

More arms may be handy for the driver, but the pedestrian is another matter. Extremities are a handicap. When he is hit by a car they tend to be broken or contused.

The ideal pedestrian, I suggest, should be almost completely spherical. He should have the minimum extension of arms and legs to enable him to trundle about and perform necessary daily tasks, but these should retract on impact so that he would roll when struck.

Since most of us are pedestrians at times, motorists at other times, it obviously would be a bad idea to design two different types of people. All these matters would have to be threshed out.

No matter what Detroit decides to do, we'll never really be safe in these outmoded bodies.

❖❖❖❖❖

Home Is Where the Umbrella Is

The superannuated friend told me when he retired some months ago that the best thing about his new life-style was that he was no longer fragmented.

"While you are working," he said, "you are divided between your home and your job. To put it simply, a man never knows where his umbrella is."

"And you think," I asked him, "that retirement will solve this problem?"

"Of course," he said. "I am operating from only one base

now, the little home. That is where the umbrella is. Where else could it be? During the years of my gainful employment, I would start out the front door, it would be raining, and the umbrella would be at the office. Conversely, if I left the job during an evening downpour, it always happened that the umbrella was at home."

"Is that why retired people are usually drier than others?" I asked.

"You are being facetious," he said, "but if my theory is correct, then that condition would naturally follow. However, the umbrella is only a small part of the total picture."

"I hope so," I said.

"For example," he went on, "if you have an old friend in Seattle or Bridgeport, one of those towns, as many people do, the chances are that you have his telephone number at work and his address at home.

"It always works out, according to some inscrutable law, that when you want to call him it's always when you are at home without his number, while if you want to write him it is when you are at work without his address."

"You could always call your wife and ask her for his address," I pointed out, "unless you don't have your wife's phone number at the office."

"Wives," he said impatiently, "are always out working at a second job so you can have enough money to retire and consolidate all your belongings, records, and impedimenta under one roof. Retirement is going to simplify things."

Naturally I wished him well, and when I saw him some time later I asked how the new system was working out.

"To be frank," he said, "not too well. All the advantages were there, as I thought they would be, but they are outweighed.

"The trouble is that when you have reduced your desk drawers, files, and so on to only one location you lose opportunities for alibis."

I urged him to explain.

"It used to be," he said, "that when your wife asked you if you had found out where the Hoopers' daughter lived so that you could send a present to their grandchild, as she had told you to do a week ago, you could say, 'Why of course I did. But I left it in my desk at work.' How could she argue with you? Then the next day you could get the information from old Hoop and nobody the wiser. The way it is now I have to admit I forgot about it.

"Looking back over the years I realize how much money I saved by saying that I would be glad to buy whatever I was being pressured about, but that my checkbook was at home, or at work, whichever served my purpose.

"Or my wife would say, 'Why don't you ever wear that plaid vest I bought you for your birthday?' and I could get out of it by telling her I wore it every day at the office and had left it hanging there in a fit of inadvertence.

"But no longer."

"Well," I said, in an effort to cheer him up, "at least you know where your umbrella is."

He sneezed.

"I certainly do," he said. "I left it at a Golden Age meeting."

❖❖❖❖

Spring Training

The Skipper of the Phictitious Phantoms squinted in the bright sunlight of the training camp. The assembled press was asking him to slake the thirst for knowledge about his team which was parching their readers up North.

"How does it look?" he was asked. "How do things shape up?"

They were the same questions that came up every spring and he knew that there was no way of answering them except in code.

And so he spoke in that strange language which we have come to recognize as Spring Training English. About all the sportswriters could do was take it down and hope that the fans back home would know how to translate it.

They knew this was expecting an awful lot from the fans, because getting at the real meaning of a training camp phrase is not an exact science.

"Well," said the Skipper, "I can say one thing, we'll be in contention."

Most authorities agree that this means: "We won't win."

Of course no manager who thinks he is going to win is allowed to make a flat prediction to that effect. He may be allowed to go as far as, "We're the ones they'll have to beat."

When you learn to look for the nuances you realize that the manager who says his team is the one to beat is more confident than the one who says that his club will be in contention. At least two or three places more confident.

If the Skipper has said, "We'll be in contention, but every club in the league has improved," it would have meant that he figured to finish last.

The Skipper was being more direct than many managers. There are those who say that they intend to play one game at a time. Even people who have devoted their lives to trying to decipher vernal pronouncements of this type aren't sure what meaning is hidden in the prediction that the season will be played one game at a time.

An educated guess is that it merely means the poor man would rather not think about the season at all.

Asked whether he was impressed by his new catcher, Fireplug Fenstermacher, the Skipper said yes he was impressed with him.

"He has a strong arm and works well with the pitchers," he

said. The sportswriters knew this was merely a polite way of saying the kid can't hit.

The Skipper is a kind and polite man. The sportswriters recognize that fact, and often refer to him as one of the real gentlemen of the game.

The Skipper wishes they wouldn't call him that. It makes him nervous. Every time he is called one of the real gentlemen of the game he gets this feeling that he is about to be fired, and he's usually right.

How does the pitching look?

The Skipper said that the veteran lefty, Ace Doozy, might make a comeback this year.

"He's working on a third pitch to add to his repertoire," the Skipper said. (Translation: He's lost his other two.)

He added that he wasn't quite set on his rotation yet. (Translation: He only has one pitcher who can get the ball over the plate.)

As for the crop of rookies, the Skipper said he was enthusiastic about them and that they would all get a chance to show what they can do. (For the next four years in Pocatello.)

As I said this is an imprecise art, and others may object to the accuracy of some of these translations, but it is a fascinating study.

And then, sometimes, managers will, for a change of pace, throw in a sentence which means just what it appears to mean. The Skipper is no exception.

"Anything can happen between now and October," he said.

And there's no reason to doubt that he meant it.

Watch for Fallen Beer Can

The editorial page of *The New York Times*, which always seems to lag behind me, has taken belated notice of my suggestion that the problem of roadside litter might be ameliorated by the introduction of the edible beer can.

It also goes on to repeat, as if it were its own, my proposal of some years back that beer cans be produced in colors and designs vernal, autumnal, or brumal, so as to melt imperceptibly into the seasonal vegetation. (I don't know the corresponding word for summer, but it doesn't make any difference. In summer I think it is best for beer cans to look frankly like beer cans. This is the time of year when people are accustomed to seeing beer cans, and to camouflage them might be a blow to traffic safety, with drivers darting their eyes hither and yon trying to locate the beer cans that they know must be out there somewhere, instead of keeping them fixed upon the road.)

The *Times* does not touch upon my plan to magnetize beer cans so that they would cling to the surface of the car from which they were flug. To develop the idea a bit further, how about a beer can in the shape of a boomerang, which would wing its way home to the litter chap who had thrown it?

(I do not like the word "litterbug." Why should the sloppiness of Man be unloaded on insects, whom I have always found, disregarding the few mavericks in any group, to be a very neat type of people?)

I have even toyed with the idea of having motorized trash receptacles whizzing about the highways. There are those who feel that the neatest bit of courtesy of all is to drop the beer can into any passing convertible or sports car, leaving it to be whisked to wherever people in convertibles and sports cars go.

The trouble is that there is some thinking that drivers of convertibles and sports cars have their rights like anybody else. Be that as it may, the rag tops button up in winter and are not available as trash receptacles.

What I have in mind is a fleet of motorcycles or little Post Office Department kind of trucks with open side cars. They would come alongside and solicit your debris. On Christmas you might stick a dollar bill or at least a greeting card in the beer can in appreciation for the service.

But it occurs to me that the entire approach may be wrong. There is something about being preached at that goes against the American grain. Particularly on the subject of littering. After all, when our forefathers made their way across the land in their covered wagons they tossed out ladder-back chairs and iron soap kettles at every opportunity, as is attested by the prevalence of antique stores along their route.

A sign that says "No Littering" merely offends something deep within us.

If we want to get rid of the beer cans, what we need is a Presidential Advisory Commission to Encourage Littering.

The Secretary of the Interior and perhaps the Ford Foundation and, if possible, *The New York Times*, should announce that the beer cans by the roadside are part of our national heritage and must be preserved.

"No pack of so-called alleged Harvard pinks who never met a payroll is going to tell me what to do with my beer cans," your Uncle Ed will shout, and he will put his beer cans in the pockets of his coat just to keep them from being federalized.

Signs along the roadside will say, the way the wildflower placards do now: "These beer cans belong to you. Do not pick them." Whole carloads of tourists with fat ladies in toreador pants and children of varying sizes will descend upon the beer cans and fill up the trunk with them and drive off with wild chortles and triumphant glee.

Whoever is in charge of the program to bring foreign visitors to our shores should point out that these folks will expect to see beer cans by the roadside. They have read about them. Beer cans will be as important to them as the Grand Canyon or Disneyland.

The well-conditioned citizen will say to himself that no bureaucrat is going to make him throw beer cans around just for the sake of some foreigner who is probably from some country nobody ever heard of but is getting his hard-earned tax dollars. And he will toss the beer can into his wife's purse before he will contribute it to the scenery.

Why Me?

From what I read I get the feeling that I am some sort of marked man, set aside for a particular alienation from the mainstream of American Life.

The trouble, briefly, is that things work for me. Generally speaking.

My telephone calls go through.

Plumbers are available and are nice guys and charge what seem to me to be reasonable amounts.

Television repairmen let me off the hook for about a tenth of what the scarifying experiences of friends and neighbors lead me to expect.

If minor appliances go wrong, the company honors its warranty.

Airlines don't lose my baggage. Planes, when I am on them, never circle the field for hours before diverting to Montreal.

Even though Ralph Nader says the chances are slim, I seem to encounter doctors who have been to medical school and paid attention.

All this is happening right here in Twentieth Century

America where, I am constantly being told, nothing works right, where carpenters don't make house calls, and the consumer is subjected to a constant Chinese water torture of rude clerks and sleazy craftsmanship.

It's an eerie feeling, I tell you.

Why me?

You are saying to yourselves, Well this is a mighty smug and complacent fellow who is riding for a terrible come-uppance.

But that's just the point. I take no pride nor comfort in this state of affairs. It is like being a fat man in a famine; people look at you oddly. You feel left out of things.

Suppose I am in a lively group where the bright chatter consists of swapping horror stories about how much it cost to get the furnace fixed and suspicions that more has been done than was necessary. Everyone chips in with his experience along those lines, or that of his Uncle Ed in Des Moines.

What can I contribute? The guy came out and looked at the furnace, kicked it a couple of times, put in a $1.25 valve and said he thought it was good for a few more years.

I can't talk about that. It's un-American.

You meet somebody and even before he starts complaining about his new refrigerator he wants to tell you about the lemon of a car he bought, with the transmission falling out in the dealer's driveway and they wouldn't do a thing about it.

Now that's interesting.

I buy medium-priced cars and they run pretty well. What problems they have are usually traceable to something I have done, such as hitting the side of the garage.

What kind of citizen does that make me when I can't de-nounce the shoddy workmanship of Detroit?

I even get along with computers. This is the ultimate blasphemy against the No. 1 essential of the American Credo, which is that if a computer can possibly foul something up it will.

Computers keep my bank account straighter than I ever did, they even refund me money I have overpaid the stores, and they seldom send me more than two copies of the same magazine.

There are those who will say I am lucky, but I can't see it that way. It is a terribly lonely feeling, being a stranger in your native land.

There is an economic factor too. Men and women are making big money writing articles describing the terrible collapse of quality in goods and services in this country. I'd like to get in on it. What editor would print a piece from a satisfied consumer? Forget it.

I tell you I would welcome it if a few things went wrong, if a few artisans were surly or tried to gyp me. I would welcome it (up to about $37 worth) as a sign that I was at last sharing the experiences which everybody else says they are undergoing.

Of course I would hate to think that the industrial/commercial complex was saving me up for a really big catastrophe.

❖❖❖❖

Dad Awakens to Obsolescence

As a man's family grows older he realizes that he has devoted a great part of his life to acquiring skills that are no longer in demand, and it is a sad awakening.

Declining use of his name, a friend says that Easter brought the fact home to him.

"In all modesty," he said proudly, "I was one of the all-time all-timers in the Easter egg field. If there were an Easter Egg Hall of Fame I would be a cinch for enshrinement. A legend in my own time is the way I, in all modesty, like to think of myself.

"I was an ovoid Titian, a cackleberry El Greco. I started out as a primitive, of course, being largely untaught in the art. Nothing but solid colors, if you know what I mean. Then I branched out into the use of those little decals that come with the coloring kit. I was feeling my way in the medium. The wax crayon for writing the children's names on the eggs was soon added to my technical arsenal as I gained confidence.

"Within a few years I was dyeing one egg two colors, and by the time I had reached full mastery of my talent was turning out three-color and even four-color eggs. Anyone who has ventured into this frontier of egg decoration will know the patience, the sureness of hand, the purity of vision that is involved in producing the multicolored Easter delight.

"Before long I was making little paper hats for the eggs and drawing faces on them and adding tufts of cotton for hair, mustaches, and beards. During the Eisenhower years my portrait of the President on an egg was the annual wonder of the neighbors, several of whom suggested that I send one to the White House or possibly out to Abilene for the library, but I never got around to it. A Lyndon Johnson egg would have been a challenge, but I would, I am convinced in all modesty, have succeeded in obtaining the likeness which eluded Peter Hurd.

"But the L.B.J. era came too late. The children lost interest in my Easter artistry, even though I was beginning to make some exciting breakthroughs in applying op and pop designs. So here I am in the full tide of my genius with no demand for my work.

"Because the Easter egg, while it is pure art, requires an audience. The Easter egg partakes of elements of McLuhanism; the medium is very much the message. It communicates, and one can't communicate when there is no one to communicate with. The children became bored with my Easter eggs, then restless, then actively rebellious. I had the feeling that if I had kept it up one more year they would have picketed me.

"I was also one of the great ones at hiding the eggs after they had been dyed. As the kids became older I discovered more and more sophisticated hiding places. There were years when I hid the eggs so cleverly that even I didn't find them all until about the middle of June.

"Many of the skills which a father develops seem to center around holidays, and they all become obsolescent as the family ages. He is no longer the only one who can put the star on the top of the Christmas tree. In fact, he is restrained from doing so because his tottering perch on a stepladder alarms the children who can quite easily reach the top of the tree while standing flat on the floor, or even kneeling.

"In the days of the unsafe, insane Fourth of July I was the only one trusted with setting off the firecrackers, lighting them with great panache from the glowing end of the cigar. Now the doctors have banned cigars, the community has outlawed firecrackers, and the kids are somewhere else anyway.

"It is suggested that there will be grandchildren for whom I can perform. I refuse. Let their own fathers learn these skills the way I did, and let them know the bitterness of the common human experience of seeing their hard-won artistry finally relegated to the shelf."

"You have your memories," I told him.

"Yes," he said, "and a dozen hardboiled eggs which I had ready in case anybody asked me to dye them. But nobody did."

MAY

May Day?

Of all the year's festive occasions, it must be admitted that May Day comes closest to being a complete flop.

The big difficulty probably is that May Day needs some new traditions or its very name is going to be remembered, if at all, only as an international distress signal. Who dances around Maypoles any more? No one in my set. Probably the reason for the decline of this lovely old celebration is that the traditional costume has pretty much disappeared.

Maypoles, in my memory at least, are properly danced around by the girls' gym class, attired in middy blouse, bloomers, long black stockings, and sneakers. Could you get a modern gym class into that getup? Probably not. And, with the participants dressed in anything else, all the romance would be gone from Maypole-dancing-around. The decline of the middy-blouse-and-bloomer spelled the ruin of the Maypole, just as surely as the abandonment of knickers killed off mumblety-peg. It's too obvious to be mere coincidence.

Or take that other great May Day custom—going a-Maying. Does your circle of friends include anyone who a-Mays? My own opinion is that people wouldn't a-May even if they knew what it was.

In medieval England people used to rush out into the forests and bring back branches of trees and armfuls of flowers.

This would give the modern American no particular charge. He (or rather his wife) does it all the time, in spite of laws against it. The first of May is no different in that respect than any other. Where is the thrill in going a-Maying if you have already been an-Aprilling and intend to go a-Juning?

Farmers, seeking to preserve their trees, simply put up "No Trespassing" signs; it is significant that they don't feel it necessary to post "A-Mayers Will Be Prosecuted."

Then there is the Queen of the May. This was a big thing. Village maidens used to issue instructions at bedtime, viz., "Come and wake me early, wake me early, mother dear, for I am to be Queen of the May."

Village maidens these days wouldn't get up early to meet Mick Jagger at the airport much less to be queen of the May. And, if they would, their mothers would tell them to get their own breakfast and not to make a lot of noise on their way out.

Moreover, when a village maiden has a chance to be Miss Cranberry Bog of 1980, Queen of Better Plumbing Week, or Sweetheart of the Gum Spirits of Turpentine Industry, all with a complete wardrobe and a trip to Nassau (aboard a luxurious DC-112) she couldn't care less about being May queen, which isn't going to get her anything more than a garland or two swiped out of somebody's garden.

Look at how trick-or-treat saved Halloween when it was just about finished. Surely something similarly appealing could rescue May 1.

The Pleasures of Ornithology

One of the great things about getting out where Nature has not been trammeled is that you can observe the birds. Two or more people can sit amid the trees, power poles, and fence posts of the forest primeval, and if they concentrate on the birds, they will find themselves in peaceful communion with one another, with all the bitterness, hatred, and pressures of the workaday world only a dim and unpleasant memory.

I was in such a mood the other day as I sat, overlooking an Ozarks lake, while smoking an afternoon pipe, with the stem of which, having removed it from my mouth, I pointed and remarked to a friend who is a highly touted amateur of ornithology, "That little long-tailed, small-headed bird which is perched upon the clothesline, what sort of rare species would you take him to be?"

"Where do you see this bird," he asked, "which sounds like either a long-tailed nithead or a nit-headed longtail, two separate birds, although often mistaken for each other."

"Just over the peak of the well house there," I said, "between the red bathing suit and the dish towel."

He consulted the library of Audubon and other authorities on the birds which he keeps constantly at his elbow, then trained his binoculars on the bird. I rate bird watchers by the size of their binoculars and this man is a very big binocular indeed.

He looked at it carefully, riffled some pages in his guidebooks, gazed again, put down the binoculars, sighed, and said, "That is a clothespin."

"Really," I said. "I had no idea they migrated this far north."

"They don't migrate," he said.

"Then," I asked, "how did it get on your clothesline?"

"My wife put it there," he said. "It is a common wooden clothespin."

"Not a rare bird then?"

"Not even a bird, old friend," he said patiently. "Just a clothespin, as any knucklehead could have plainly seen."

A silence fell as I told myself how pleasant it was to be engaged in this peaceful discussion of the beauties of Nature, far from the marts of trade where men argue, bicker, and fight over pieces of paper and coins of what used to be silver.

"Old friend," I said at last, "if you will look over there between the red bathing suit and the dish towel, you will see that your clothespin has just flown away."

"Oh," he said. "That was a lesser tufted potlatch. I thought you meant that clothespin by the blue bathing suit."

"Are you color-blind?" I asked.

"You mean to imply," he retorted, "that a man who has made a career of distinguishing among birds by such matters as whether their breast is a greenish-yellow shading into a tawny umber, is color-blind?"

"You can't tell a red bathing suit from a blue bathing suit," I said.

"You can't tell a clothespin from a tufted potlatch," he snapped.

"I can now," I replied with some acerbity. "One of them can fly."

His face flushed and he bit angrily at his lip.

"I just saw a raspy-throated finch," he cried. "And you didn't."

"What makes you think I didn't see him?" I said.

"Because," he said, "birds hate to be watched by ignoramuses who voted for Gerald Ford, and think that clothespins can fly."

"You may not like my politics," I said, "but at least I don't go around making stupid remarks about inflation. Lend me your binoculars."

"I won't," he said, "you'll break them like you broke my camera."

"That was in 1967."

"You see," he said triumphantly, "every ten years you break something of mine. Anyway I don't want an idiot who doesn't know anything about birds watching my birds, and what's so stupid about my remarks about inflation?"

So I told him and he went into the cabin and slammed the door, and I'm afraid we may have to reconsider our thinking on the peace-making qualities of a shared love of Nature.

(Note: The names of all birds mentioned have been changed to protect the innocent. Except for the clothespin.)

❖❖❖❖

"...And That Spells Mother...."

Q—You are a mother?

A—Boy, you polltakers are getting smarter all the time. You wade up to the door through twenty feet of tricycles, scooters, buggies, and roller skates; there's a clothesline full of tiny garments right in plain view; I'm holding what any fairly perceptive human being could identify as a baby; and you ask me if I'm a mother?

Q—Are you a typical mother?

A—You want a fat lip, mister? You want to talk to a typical mother, go see the duchess next door. She's the typical mother. One kid and a full-time maid.

Q—This makes her typical?

A—Well, it makes her look like the typical mother that I see in the ads, who's always showing her husband how clean she got the kid's clothes with some soap or other. Those things kill me. Here you see this gal who's obviously spent the day in the beauty parlor. Which is O.K. I'm not knocking it. I wish I had the time. Anyway, she gets all fixed up for her old man and he comes home, maybe after a hard day at the wherever, and would like to have a cold beer and listen to the ball game. She drags out little Leroy's shirt.

"See, Harold," she says, "how fresh, clean, and sweet-smelling little Leroy's shirt is."

In the ads the husband says, "My, what a clever little manager lucky me married."

In real life what would he say—or, anyway, what would my old man say? "I didn't come home to smell no laundry. How come there's only one cold beer?"

These typical mothers really do me in.

"Dr. Tuckerman," they say to the dentist, "I am concerned about Lily Belle. She will not brush her teeth up and down."

She goes to the dentist to tell him this. It's a wonder she didn't call him at two a.m. and get sore because he doesn't make night calls.

Another thing they do is when the dog comes in with its muddy paws and jumps in the clean laundry. They smile and shake their heads and say, "Bad Doggy."

If that flea-bearing freeloader of ours ever pulled that trick it would be the sorriest day of his mangy life.

Q—Could you make your answers a little briefer? The blanks on this form are really quite small.

A—So shove off—who asked you anyway?

Q—No, no. It's quite all right. I just have a few more questions. What do you think of Mother's Day?

A—I think it's great. I sent my mother a wire.

Q—Splendid; what was the sentiment?

A—"Come quick; I'm going nuts."

Q—Will she come?

A—Sure. She's my mom.

Q—You do approve of motherhood, then?

A—I gave up Hollywood for it, didn't I?

Q—Hollywood?

A—Hollywood, North Dakota. It's one of my husband's little jokes.

Q—In the papers the other day there was a story about a mother who saved her child from injury by singlehandedly lifting a station wagon under which the little rascal was pinned. Do you think you could do the same for one of yours?

A—I'd have to. The mister has a slipped disk.

Q—Yes. Now as a mother do you love your children? Do you tenderly nurture them, look out for their wants, guide them on the right path, warm them with your maternal affection?

A—Yeah. Sure. What else can you do with kids?

Q—You feel, don't you, that Mother's Day should be observed the year around?

A—You mean that I should get five handkerchiefs and a handwoven potholder every day all year?

Q—Not necessarily. I mean that mothers should be appreciated the year around. Don't you think so?

A—Mister, I'm appreciated about all I can stand as it is. From five a.m. until nearly midnight, it's "Maw, I'd appreciate it if you'd iron my dress" or "Maw, I'd appreciate it if you'd hit us a few grounders." Just one day without any appreciation, that's what I need.

Q—You know what I think?

A—No, and I don't much care.

Q—I think you're a typical mother.

A—Get out of here before I find something heavier than this baby to hit you with.

❖❖❖❖

Pomp and Circumstance

All the years of schooling culminate for the young American in the commencement address. Here is where it comes to a focus. In about forty-five minutes, the distinguished orator gives the class the distilled wisdom of the ages and launches them upon the sea of life.

If the graduates will listen closely, this is what they will learn:

1. Although the world faces many problems, these are exciting times to be alive. The reason these are exciting times is because of these very problems. The speaker personally wishes he were as young as these fine young Americans because then he, too, could participate in the excitement and, well, yes, challenge of the years ahead.

2. We read too much about the disco freaks and the marijuana users and the flaunters of dirty words and LSD. Well, the speaker believes, this is what sells newspapers. As a matter of fact, he wishes that people who write these things could be here today and look across this broad sea of intelligent, clean American faces. Then these people would realize that the radicals and the drop-outs are only a small minority.

3. The world outside these ivied halls is different than the world inside these ivied halls. Out there the world has no patience with the man or woman who settles for a mere "passing" grade. It is very competitive out there, the speaker feels.

4. The speaker is amused by recalling that when he graduated he thought he knew all the answers. This, he discovered, was not true. To be frank, the students are only beginning the process of education. That is why this ceremony is called a com-mence-ment. They may think that they are educated now, but the man or woman who ceases to expand his horizons, to think creatively, to exercise his brain will soon fall behind in the race of life.

5. When he was young the speaker was very poor. He did not have the many advantages which an affluent society has bestowed upon the class assembled here today. He knows the view is unpopular, but it is his personal opinion that it was those early hardships which molded his character and car-

ried him to the pinnacle of success upon which he now stands. The pioneers, whom he deeply admires, were quite a bit like him in that respect.

6. It is the speaker's impression that the old-fashionable virtues of honesty, decency, and regular bathing are now considered "square." If so, then he is proud to be square, because he has personally observed that his own lifelong devotion to honesty, decency, and regular bathing has paid off.

7. Liberty is not the same as license, rights involve responsibilities, and free speech does not entitle a man to holler "Fire," in a crowded theater.

8. Man's scientific progress is moving ahead in leaps and bounds. Major breakthroughs are at hand. And yet, the sober truth is that man's social and ethical progress is failing to keep up. The speaker agrees with all other thinking men that this is a bad thing.

9. While the speaker is not so vain as to believe that the members of the class will remember everything he has said here today, he does not feel the day will have been wasted if some remark of his will be of assistance to you young Americans as you go through life. They are, after all, things that he himself learned in work and study over more years than he cares to think about.

10. A sense of humor is a wonderful thing because it enables us to laugh at ourselves.

11. The speaker is reminded of a joke in closing.

With these golden words ringing in their heads the graduates go out from the ivied halls almost unable to walk under the burden of all that wisdom.

❖❖❖❖

HOTEL

Do you remember the olden days when we country boys would come to town and there would be this gas lamp in the hotel room and, having never seen the like, we would blow it out and there would be all the resultant asphyxiation? Or we had never seen electricity and would cut the cord leading to the light bulb?

Of course you remember all that, and you think we are too sophisticated any more to be unable to cope with the wonders of a hotel room. But don't bet on it.

Today the hotel room is so complex you can't run it without an instruction manual and a thirty-minute lecture by the bellman.

The guy that carries the grip used to come in, turn on the light, open a couple of doors, showing the closet and the bathroom, put the key on the dresser, pocket his tip and exit merrily.

But no longer. Instead he calls sternly for attention and goes over the room, explaining every pushbutton and dial, from the thermostat to the machine that makes the ice cubes. He has to tell you which ones it is O.K. for the layman to touch and which ones to let alone. It would be an exaggeration to say that it is a briefing as complete as that given the astronauts, but it comes pretty close.

And the guest had better pay attention.

I was spending the night in a hotel awhile back, and I felt that I could sleep better if the television weren't blatting. I have seen a television set before and I felt that I was competent to turn one off. I pushed, pulled, or twisted everything that protruded from the box. It went serenely on. I was reduced to the final humiliation. I called the desk to admit that I hadn't paid close attention to the instructions, or had anyway failed to take notes.

Where you had to turn the television off was a switch set

into the head of the bed. Very convenient, of course, but also confusing to a man who had come to terms with television sets on the basis that they had an On-Off switch somewhere on their chassis, not clear across the room.

Also, telephoning the desk isn't the simple thing it once was. You have to have a pretty accurate idea of what you want. There is one number for the valet and another for room service and another for reservations, and so on. It's no longer a matter of picking up the phone and telling the nice lady you want a chicken sandwich, your suit pressed, and an outside line.

You have to study the fine print before you dare lay a finger on the dial.

As I have said, if you miss one syllable of the bellman's lecture you can end up with a temperature of 97 degrees in the room, or you'll find out at two o'clock in the morning that the ice machine has filled the bathtub with cubes and shows no signs of quitting.

The flight instructor who shows you to your room—and often he doesn't even carry the luggage, that's handled by another subsidiary—will inquire, "Have you stayed with us before, sir?"

If, like me, you are the type who tries to bluff through situations of this kind by pretending to a sophistication you don't possess, you will say, "Oh, yes, I have stayed with you incessantly. Do you take me for some sort of huckleberry or other?"

Often the uniformed chap is kind enough not to just walk away and leave you in your ignorance, as he might well do. Instead he will ask, "All right then, wise guy, sir, where's the bed?"

You look around confidently, assuming that even you can find a bed in a hotel room. There's no bed.

"That's funny," you say. "I must have stayed in a different kind of room last time."

"They're all alike," he says.

"Do I get three guesses?" you ask.

By this time he is weary of the game and shows you what article of furniture the bed pops out of if you know the combination. There is a round of winks, chuckles, and tips, and about midnight when you get ready to go to bed you have to call somebody or other and ask where they hide the pillows.

The modern hotel room is a wonder of comfort and convenience. Living in one is no more difficult than flying a four-engine jet. But, in both cases, you'd better get all the expert advice possible before you try to operate one on your own.

❖❖❖❖

I Got the Horse Right Here...

I feel that I shouldn't pay any attention to the Kentucky Derby this year. I have not, as we say in so many disparate fields these days, paid my dues.

The thing is that for years I have gone along not knowing the name of one horse from another. Then the first Saturday in May rolls around and suddenly I am Nathan Detroit, putting my fifty cents in the office pool and even trapping neighbors into wagering a quarter.

I read the paper the morning of the Derby and find out the names of the horses. They are all strange to me, but by the time the race comes around I am a walking encyclopedia of lore about who is a good mudder and who isn't, and have even refreshed my memory as to the difference between a fetlock and a furlong (an interesting study in itself).

If it is not too late I would like to say that I am ashamed of behaving this way. I realize that I have not been involved in horse racing on a day-to-day basis the way some of my friends are.

There may be a similarity here to the man who drinks only on New Year's Eve. He is treated with understandable coolness by those who have been buying mink coats for the distillers' wives on a year-round basis.

So the horseplayer who studies the form charts whenever the bangtails (which I believe is the word) are running probably resents the intrusion of amateurs into his own private world when the Run for the Roses grips the attention of the sportsminded world.

Perhaps an even more pertinent comparison is the way people who have never given a thought to politics suddenly appear out of nowhere into the here when an election is afoot.

The man who pays attention to public affairs only once every four years cannot be accepted as a serious citizen by those who agonize over everything from the farm program to Far East policy on a full-time basis.

There is a suspicion that these quadrennial pols are only in it for the publicity involved in making bets that will require the loser to push a peanut down Main Street with his nose.

Under our system of government the man who has never rung a doorbell or attended a ward meeting is entitled to emerge as a political voice when an election brings glamour to what is otherwise a workaday business.

And, of course, I am guaranteed the right, even though it may not be spelled out in the Constitution, to notice horse racing only when the mint julep and "My Old Kentucky Home" bring the sport to my attention.

But this year I have mustered the decency to abstain. I am leaving the Derby to those who have earned the right to be interested in it by their support of the track in its more humdrum moments. For me to care about the Derby would be as hypocritical as for a man who hasn't been to a movie in two years to watch the awarding of the Oscars.

All of us who are right-thinking disdain those "celebrities" who occupy the boxes at the World Series without having paid their way into a ball park all season long.

So, at the risk of seeming unduly noble, I will return the Derby to the horseplayers who have proven their devotion to what has, on occasion, been called the Sport of Kings.

Besides, I'll be saving the seventy-five cents that those pools annually suck down the drain. The opportunity to be both noble and cheap doesn't come around every day.

JUNE

Conservation Brings Back Conversation

If people are really as concerned about the decline of conversation as they keep saying they are, then what they should do is abolish air conditioning. In the Middle West we used to have grand conversations from Memorial Day until the first frost about how we were managing to bear up under the heat.

"Well," a fellow would say, "I drug the mattress around the house until along about three a.m. I put it in a corner of the kids' room and this little bit of air come trickling in over the windowsill and I got some sleep."

There was always one conversationalist who would say that at his house there was always a breeze.

"Always a breeze," he would say. "Why, lots of nights when people have said it was stifling I have had to pull up the top sheet before midnight."

People would admire him and ask what part of town he lived in, and when he told them they would say that, yes, they had heard there was always a nice breeze around there, probably because it was situated so high.

The conversationalist would say that was very true. It was because his house was on a sort of hill so that the breeze—if there was one, and there generally was—could sweep right in his window unimpeded.

It all made for good, lively talk when one man could tell that he always took the hose and sprinkled the house every evening. This would turn out to be controversial, and somebody else would say sprinkling the house did no good.

But everybody would listen to everybody else's ideas, no matter how nutty they might be. Feelings would run a little high, but there was always a little central area of agreement. People would chime in with "That's right" and "Very true" when someone, a sort of peacemaker in the group, would say, "I don't mind how hot it gets as long as I can get my sleep."

Keeping the sheets in the icebox right up until bedtime was a theory with many adherents.

Occasionally the conversation would become especially piquant when a lady would admit that she kept her girdle in the icebox overnight so as to be able to make a cool start in the morning. Often there would be interesting discussions as to whether it was better to keep the place shut up all day long, with the shades down, or to open everything up. Families were riven down the middle on this matter.

There were those who would argue that a southeast exposure was the only bearable one, and others would take a diametrically opposite view.

I'll tell you, those were the lively days. Nobody talks about the weather any more because so many have done something about it. If you don't have at least a little old wheezy box in the window, why, you keep quiet about it because everybody else has been refrigerated all night long and wouldn't know what you were talking about.

Even in the automobiles now there is likely to be an arctic blast from the dashboard and nobody wants to hear about how you drove across Kansas with a wet towel around your neck and one foot in a bucket of ice water.

It's nice, of course, to think about coolness becoming more

and more widespread among our people, but it has sure ruined small talk.

❖❖❖❖❖

June

One person who is insensitive to the inner sweetness of my soul sneers that one good thing about June is that not even I could write anything bad about it.

Which just proves that this person is not only insensitive but wrong. It would be no great trick to make uncomplimentary observations about June.

But it would be uncommercial; it wouldn't sell.

The great poets understood this. By the great poets I mean the ones who lived in nice houses around Concord or places like that, where the school children came to see them on their birthdays and put laurel wreaths on their pates and everybody strolled over to the nearest Howard Johnson's for ice cream.

These poets had nothing but good things to say about June.

Now as for the fellows who were toiling away in garrets, dipping their pens in vitrol and worse, well we will never know what they thought about June. If we wish to waste our time thinking about these drudges we can assume that they put the knock on June and no editor would touch their verse with a ten-foot rejection slip.

My own private theory is that no month is intrinsically better or worse than any other. It's just that some were lucky enough to get superior public relations advice. June's P.R. counsel is the best in the business. It must make it the envy of the other months.

If June were to run for public office it would be the ideal candidate. It looks great on television. The cigarette people recognized the fact. It was always June in the cigarette commercials.

And the people who handle June have seen to it that it is associated with weddings and commencement exercises and other pleasant occasions. Prominent in its image are young creatures out in the fields, trembly-legged colts and baby lambs and similar ilk. How could anybody fault a month that produces so many scenes that trigger the cuteness response which lies within even the sternest innards?

If months were used cars, the legend on the windshield of June would be "Cream Puff."

It is a masterful job of selling. No other month comes close.

And yet, as I have said, it wouldn't be too difficult to spot some flaws. It is a month of floods and tornadoes and tropical storms.

If you estimate your federal income tax there is a payment due.

If it is the month of weddings it is also the month of wedding presents to be bought and of wedding receptions featuring interminable reception lines, with warm punch and a handful of peanuts (cashews if you're lucky) as a reward.

If it brings the joys of the commencement ceremony it also provides the agony of the commencement speech, and the thrill of accomplishment closely followed by the hunt for a job.

There is, knee-deep in June, the release of vacation time, but also the bitter realization that once again you aren't going to be able to afford any of the things you really want to do.

June busts out all over with growing things. But those same growing things have to be pruned and mowed and sprayed and plucked out from the cracks in the sidewalks. It brings the song of the birds, but also the hum of the mosquito and the bitter malevolence of the chigger.

Dance barefoot across the flower-speckled hills of June if

you wish, but look out for the poison ivy.

I could mention all these things, but I won't. The image of June has been too firmly impressed upon us by the skilled manipulators of opinion. Even if we can accept, intellectually, that June is not perfect, we reject the idea emotionally.

She is such a pretty, giddy month, is June, that nobody holds her responsible for the things that happen while she is around.

The person who said that not even I could find fault with June is half wrong. I could. But he (or rather she) is also half right. I'm not going to.

❖❖❖❖

You're Joking!

I made up a joke the other night, lying there in the early morning hours when the middle-aged man searches the dark resources of his soul for something interesting to think about.

I had never made up a joke before. I had never known anybody who had made up a joke. I have made remarks of humorous intent but never a joke.

The way you can identify a joke is that it begins. "There was this fellow, see, have you heard it?"

The joke is more formally structured than the witticism, the aphorism, or the pungent comment. It has to have a beginning, a middle, an end, and a cast of characters.

My assumption had been that jokes were not thought up, they were inherited. Now, of course, I have revised old jokes in a new form, which usually involves cleaning them up, but that is not creativity; that is tinkering.

Before I tell you this joke, if I ever do, I had better explain what kind of joke this is. I have seen it called a triple pun, but I'm not sure that the description is accurate.

What it is is a particular kind of joke which some people love and which leads others to lie down in a dark room with a cool cloth.

There were a lot of these jokes going around in My Set the last week. So all right, I'll give you an example.

There was this poet, Percy Bysshe Shelley, who had died and gone to heaven. While he was standing in line, waiting for admittance, a nun, standing in front of him, asked him to hold her place while she went to get a drink of water and he said he would.

The line moved, and by the time the poet got to the great registry book, the sister had not returned. So he felt he might as well make the required squiggle with the goose quill.

But just as he began to write a voice thundered, "Wait 'til the nun signs, Shelley."

O.K. That's the joke.

There are many more in this genre. Some of them, if you can believe it, are even funnier. But the one about Shelley has the advantage of being short. Compared to the others, that is. Mostly these tend to be long jokes. Some of them are so long in fact that people who tell them often forget the punch lines. Others write the punch line on a piece of paper as a reminder when they approach the smash finale.

One of them ends up, "The squaw on the hippopotamus is equal to the sons of the squaws on the other two hides." I don't have the space to give it all to you, but can you imagine being hit by a car and having a slip with that line written on it found in your possession?

My joke is;

There was this fellow . . . have you heard it? . . . who owned a restaurant. He hired a toothless old Gypsy woman to mingle among the tables, playing her violin.

Now this fellow tumbled down a flight of steps leading to his living quarters over the restaurant. The fall broke both his wrists so that he was unable to shave himself.

So he asked the toothless old Gypsy lady who wandered among the customers playing the violin if she would shave him.

To which she replied, "A strolling crone lathers no boss."

Take my word for it, it's a great joke. Also I made it up all by myself.

When I finally got up the courage to try it on an assembled group they all said they'd heard it.

❖❖❖❖

F-A-T-H-E-R

I asked a young man of my acquaintance to write something sentimental for Father's Day, perhaps along the lines of the famous tribute to M-O-T-H-E-R. He has done so, but I also reserved the right to make a few comments about his composition.

F—IS FOR THE FLAB AROUND HIS MIDDLE.

Very cute. It never occurs to these young sprouts that this is honest flab, accumulated by years of slaving away at a hot desk in order to provide the wherewithal. If some people I could name had to spend thirty-five years sitting down instead of jouncing around on a trampoline or a tennis court, they might have a little honest flab to show for it.

It is true that the television and other misleading media have shown America being built by the flat-tummied, but the facts of the case might prove otherwise. My theory is that flab built this country, and don't you ever forget it. Courses in Fat Studies should be made compulsory in all our educational institutions.

A—IS FOR THE ALLOWANCE HE ALWAYS FORGOT.

Hoo-boy. Forgetting and not having are two different things. Entirely. No father wants to be $3,986.50 in arrears on the allowance. I'll accept your figures as correct, but I don't think you're ever going to collect. In fact, I'll guarantee it.

And that notation about the 10 percent interest due does credit to your mathematics teachers, but that's about all I can say for it. Those I.O.U.s that I may or may not have given you in lieu of cash will never stand up in court.

T—IS FOR HIS TERRIBLE TASTE IN TIES.

Now a word about that. No man, especially a father, should be judged by what is around his neck, unless it is a noose. Neckties are given to a man by his wife and children. They are picked out with regard to what his sons can borrow. What he ends up with in his old age are the neckties that nobody would swipe or, having once taken, give back.

This explains why fathers wear wide ties when their sons wear narrow ones or, as is now the case, vice-versa.

You cannot show your tie rack to a son and say, "Some day these will all be yours." His reply is, "Why not now?" The boy ends up with the latest in toggery and is free to make fun of his dad walking around with the preceding decade's fashions around his neck.

H—IS FOR HIS HAIRLINE THAT'S RECEDING.

All right. For some people hair is important. As you grow older you realize there is no particular mystique involved.

A lot of that hair, too, let's remember, disappeared because of the worry and stress of rearing a family. You may ask why, if this is the case, mothers, who do most of the work, don't get bald. You may also have noticed bald bachelors. You will say that I cannot blame the receding hairline on the mere fact of fatherhood. There are good answers to these questions but I can't think of them at the moment.

E—IS FOR THE ERRORS HE COMMITTED.

So, a man voted for Dewey, bought an Edsel, and predicted that Mickey Mantle would never make it in the major leagues. Wasn't I right about moss growing on the north side of trees, the cardinal being a red bird, and cigarettes being bad for you? Never mind about how much I smoke. The point is that everyone is entitled to a few mistakes. I would say that if I were perfect I would be unbearable, except that I'm not going to give you a straight line like that.

R—IS FOR HIS RUGGED CONSTITUTION.

Sarcasm ill becomes the young. Just because the time we went on an overnight hike it seemed more sensible to me to sleep in a motel than out in a field doesn't mean anything. The last man that made me sleep in a tent was Franklin D. Roosevelt. In his honor I promised not to spend the night under canvas at the suggestion of any lesser man.

Put them all together, they spell F-A-T-H-E-R.

(Thanks for the box of cigars.)

❖❖❖❖

Fear of Not Flying

Whatever we may think of the ethics of the sixteen-year-old who flew from Kansas City to London without a ticket, apparently by picking the right flights and flashing an empty loading envelope, we must be impressed by the aplomb of the generation he represents.

It is a quality which I, at least, excessively lack. Getting on an airplane is an ordeal.

In the first place, I am obsessed with the idea that I am about to miss my flight. Sitting in the coffee shop, an hour before the scheduled departure, I see a sign on the wall: "No

109

Flight Announcements." It has the same effect on me as though it said "Cholera." I gulp my coffee and rush outside where I can hear the loudspeaker, which I never understand.

It says, "Passenger Wahh W. Wahh for Wahhwahh, please come to the Wahh Wahh Airline ticket counter. Passenger Wahh."

I rush up to the nearest uniformed figure and surrender:

"What did I do wrong? I'm sorry. If there's anything extra I'll pay."

It turns out, of course, that it is not my airline or my destination and that the man they want is indeed a Passenger Wahh. I have never, incidentally, seen any of the Passengers Wahh, but they are a family that travels extensively. At least they always seem to be going somewhere on days when I am in an air terminal.

Even more chilling is when the horn says, "Wahhwahh Airlines announces the departure of its Slippery Elm Green Carpet Flight Wahh to Wahh. Leaving from Gate 9, Concourse G, Finger 112. All passengers please board."

Great Scott!

It doesn't sound like my flight, but it's leaving, while I'm standing here buying a newspaper. I don't dare take a chance. Gate 9, Concourse G, Finger 112 is so far away it's in a different time zone, so I gain an hour but I would have missed the plane even if it had been mine which, I discover, when I get there, it isn't.

Most air passengers only check in at the ticket counter once. I do it two or three times. How do I know that the last fellow who checked me in was really a ticket person? Anybody can fake a uniform. Maybe he was a sixteen-year-old boy trying to get to London.

I go back for reassurance. They get so they remember me and say that they don't have to check my ticket again. I beg them to do it anyway. The last man who stamped it was using a wornout ink pad. Suppose I get thrown off the plane because the stamp is illegible? They say there is really nothing more they need to do. I invite them to get my luggage back and weigh it again. They say it won't be necessary.

When the time comes to board the plane, I check in at the gate. The man says, "Thank you, sir," and I say, "Does this plane go to Chicago?" He says, "No, why?" and I say, "Well, so many of them do. Go to Chicago that is, and I'm not. I'm going to Los Angeles to see my sister's oldest boy who's in the hardware game."

He says this plane is going to Los Angeles, but I check it again at the foot of the gangplank with a man who has mufflers on his ears. I yell, "Los Angeles?" at him and he nods. At the top of the stairs I show my ticket to the stewardess and explain to her about the wornout rubber stamp. It's pretty noisy but she nods and says, "Wahh."

What does she mean by that? It worries me. I go up and down the aisle asking everybody if they are going to Chicago. They all say they aren't, which reassures me. But after I've asked them if they're going to Chicago they all take their tickets out and look at them again, which starts me worrying all over.

Well, of course, I get to Los Angeles all right. But it just proves one of the handicaps of being born before the age of air.

That kid stowed away easier than I can fly with a paid-up ticket.

❖❖❖❖❖

The Old Ball Game

While many perceptive observers of the social scene were predicting a bleak future for baseball a few years back, I went out on an opposite limb. I said baseball was going to grow in popularity. In fact it had to, unless this society was going to get as sick as the gloomier critics claim it already is.

I went to the ball park the other day. It was in the afternoon, which is when God intended man to play baseball. The weather was beautiful and the game moved at its ancient and stately pace.

There are those who contend that baseball is too slow. If it is, then the fault is with a civilization which cries out incessantly for more speed for speed's sake alone. We need something to slow us down. Most other sports are mining the box-office lode of continuous noise and action.

Life was not meant to be lived at a constant hyped-up pitch.

The spectator at a baseball game has time to unwind his nerves, contemplate eternal verities, and dissolve that hard knot which modern man carries around in the pit of his stomach.

Of course baseball has its touch of boredom. What worthwhile human activity doesn't? To be slightly bored is to be more receptive to the periods of heightened emotion. A fact that the composers of great symphonies fully understood.

If we want to indulge ourselves with the theory that a nation's sports reflect its character, then I guess it can be said that the games which have prospered most mightily in recent years indicate that we are, indeed, a violent lot.

The glamor spots are those which involve the crunch of bone and the thud of elbows, fists, and feet. Football and hockey inflame the jungle beast within even the sweetest of little old ladies. Basketball long since outgrew the idea that it was a non-contact sport.

No one sits quietly in a rowboat if he can stick a motor on its stern and roar off in pursuit of the wily trout. Who would think of trudging through the silent snowscape when it can be traversed at high speed and an ear-splitting noise level on a snowmobile?

Only baseball remains to remind us that leisure was meant to be spent in a leisurely manner and that we do not have to beat one another up in order to have a good time.

Well, you will say, if we are a violent country, then why weren't those who predicted the decline of baseball right? How can it compete with more violent sports? The point is that we cannot become more violent without going completely berserk. The pendulum must swing, and then baseball will return to its rightful place.

Another mark of the times has been a rejection by many elements in our society of logical reasoning, of abstract thinking, of any respect for the study of history. Anti-intellectualism is rampant on the streets.

Baseball is a game of logic. It is cerebral more than physical. Its great figures have been thinkers (of a sort) first and athletes second.

The baseball fan's enjoyment has a high intellectual content. No one can really savor fandom without a mind finely attuned to the records and statistics of the past and filled with the biographies of its heroes.

If then, as it must, the fever of contempt for all rational thought is to abate, the weary survivors will turn to baseball.

What it adds up to is that it is not baseball's responsibility to fit itself into our frantic society. It is rather society's responsibility to make itself worthy of baseball.

That's why I can never understand why anybody leaves the game early to beat the traffic. The purpose of baseball is to keep you from caring if you beat the traffic.

❖❖❖❖❖

Camera Control

Delahanty, who is into ecology and conservation these days, ordered the small pepperoni pizza and said it would be better if hunters would use cameras instead of guns.

"I'm not so sure," said Phil Plimmer, whose folks still live on the farm. "Dad wrote me that a bunch of camera nuts from the city came on his property and tore down a couple of fences without even asking his permission. Left flashbulbs all over the place. He's thinking of putting up 'No Snapshooting' signs. I'll have the cheeseburger, Rose."

"Yes," said Rose the waitress, "they got on my brother-in-law's place and one of them, some slob chewing a cigar and wearing a red hat, took a picture of my sister.

"'Why are you taking my wife's picture?' my brother-in-law asked.

"So the guy answers, 'Your wife? I thought she was a moose.' Which didn't make Sis very happy. Her husband ran off the whole bunch of them with a pitchfork."

"You're both making all this up," Delahanty said sullenly.

"Why, no," said Cromwell Boggs, who had just joined the luncheon group and put in his order for tuna supreme, easy on the mercury, "there's a lot of talk these days about the need for tighter camera control, Delahanty. I was reading an editorial about it."

"That's right," said Phil Plimmer. "I think I read the same one. It said that there were thousands of unnecessary and even painful photographs taken in this country every year. And still, anyone, even a child or a drunk or a criminal, can buy a camera with no questions asked."

"And the editorial concluded that cameras should be registered," said Cromwell Boggs, "if it's the same one I read."

"They can't do that," Delahanty snorted. "It's unconstitutional."

"You mean every citizen has a right to bear cameras?" asked Phil Plimmer. "Is that in the Constitution?"

"Delahanty wouldn't say so if it weren't," said Cromwell Boggs. "But we must remember that when the nation was established, ours was a simple agricultural society. In this increasingly complex world there must be some control on the number of cameras. Many households have regular photographic arsenals. You can't tell me the Founding Fathers would have approved of that!"

"Cameras do not take pictures," Delahanty said sententiously. "People take pictures."

"And some pretty revolting ones at that," said Phil Plimmer. "The point is that if cameras weren't so readily at hand, a lot of unfortunate pictures that are taken in the heat of anger would never happen."

"In all fairness," said Cromwell Boggs, "I must admit to a fondness for photography. I have even, on occasion, referred to myself as a camera nut. But the important thing to remember is that I learned respect for the camera from my father who bought me my first Brownie when I was but a lad. He taught me never to point the lens at myself. In fact he always said: 'Never aim a loaded camera at anything unless you intend to photograph it.' That was what he always said."

"And quite commendable of him," said Phil Plimmer. "My own father used to keep a camera in the house, but he hid the film in a different dresser drawer to avoid the snapping of accidental pictures.

"I can see no objection to requiring owners to register their hand cameras," Phil Plimmer suggested.

"That way lies dictatorship," Delahanty exploded. "History tells us that the first thing a totalitarian state does is to deprive the citizen of his camera. How would you like to live in a country where the government had all the cameras?"

He was quivering with rage.

Rose the waitress poured him another cup of coffee.

"Well," she said to Delahanty, "you let them get to you again today, didn't you?"

❖❖❖❖

Golden Age?

"Were you around in the Golden Age of Baseball?" a young friend asks.

"Yes," I snap.

"How about the Golden Age of Golf, Tennis, and Boxing?"

"Of course," I answer, "and you can throw in the Golden Age of Jai Alai."

Not only all these but I remember the Golden Age of Opera and the Golden Age of Radio, to say nothing of the Golden Age of Vaudeville and the Musical Saw, which overlapped.

Nostalgia sets in very quickly these days. Already they are talking about the Golden Age of Television, which must have been a couple of weeks when I was out of town.

If a man wants to survive he had better start storing up Golden Ages. And I am a little worried about young people today. How many Golden Ages do they have? The Golden Age of Television, yes, but what else?

It's going to be embarrassing for the kids when they age and the grandchildren come around and ask, "What about the Golden Age of ———." What?

Maybe the Golden Age of Rock-'n'-Roll. But hasn't the real Golden Age already passed? The years of Elvis Presley, Bill Haley and his Comets, and Chubby Checkers?

I'm not sure how Golden Ages are determined. Some of them may be phony, but I have experienced a Golden Age of Oratory and two or three Golden Ages of the Banjo. It's undoubtedly true that people who are passing through a Golden Age don't realize it until later when the critics have weighed everything and decided that was what it was.

Still, I can't figure out what this is the Golden Age of. It's not the Golden Age of the Movies or of Cooking or of Architecture. We've already had all those.

The Golden Age of Poetry, it's not; nor Painting, Sculpture, or Music.

116

Certainly it's not the Golden Age of Statesmanship.

Read the papers and you know it's not the Golden Age of Dress Design, of Automobiles, of the Theater, or of Journalism. There is no point in talking about the Golden Age of the Pizza, because it's not and even if it were that's a flippant aside. A true Golden Age has to be a period that sparkles in one of the major concerns of humanity.

I don't mean that we aren't making progress in every field. But can practitioners of, let's say, Medicine or the Law truthfully say that this is the Golden Age of their professions? I hope not.

This isn't even the Golden Age of Roller Skating.

It may be that we are on the threshold of the Golden Age of Space Exploration, but I wouldn't say we were in it. It's something to mark down in the futures book, like the Golden Age of Peace, which also isn't quite with us yet.

I remember the Golden Age of Billiards and of Musical Comedies. What Golden Ages will today's youngsters have to boast about?

There is no point in talking about the Golden Age of the Skateboard or of the Beard. The first instance is merely a fad, not a Golden Age, and the second doesn't exist, because the beard has had Golden Ages several hirsute miles ahead of the present one.

Will there ever be Golden Ages again? The middle-aged observer sighs and fears not. He could, however, be wrong. Golden Ages may be happening all around him and escaping his notice.

It is possible, after all, that the real Golden Age is youth and that people who are young today will find, amid what looks to me like a wallow of mediocrity, things to look back upon thirty years from now and say, "Yes, that was truly the Golden Age of ———."

I just wish I had some clue as to Golden Age of What.

JULY

The Glorious Fourth

"You poor little tads," this grandfather said the other day. "It wrings my old heart to think of you being deprived of an old-fashioned Fourth of July like we used to have. I suppose you want me to tell you about it?"

"Well," said one of his grandchildren, "I've got a skate-board lesson at four o'clock."

"This won't take long," said this grandfather. "It is the duty of every grandfather to tell about how much better things were when he was a boy so that his grandchildren will feel miserable. I am only doing my duty."

"Thank you, Grandfather," the children chorused, and there were cries of "Tell us about it!" and "Get it over with!"

"First of all," this grandfather said, "we made the ice cream. And we turned the crank and turned the crank and turned the crank."

"It sounds like fun," said one of the boys politely.

"Oh, it was wonderful," the old gentleman said. "And finally we had this wonderful peach ice cream."

"Just a minute," said the little girl with the analytical mind. "You mean after all that cranking you ended up with nothing but one icky flavor of ice cream?"

"Well, uh, yes, but—"

"Boy," various children said, "that must have been some glorious Fourth all right with no banana-fudge, no coffee-butterscotch, no pistachio-pineapple, no marshmallow-mint, no pickled pecan, no caramel-crunch, no peanut-lime, no . . ."

"We liked peach."

"Of course, Grandfather, peach is nice," said the kids, and nudged one another. "What else did you do?"

"One thing that was about the most fun was we would rent a boat and Father, your great-grandfather, would row us around the lake in Stoddard Park."

"And then what?"

"That was all. He just rowed us around."

"Hey," said one of the boys, "remember last year when we went out in the Smitherbys' ninety-seven-foot cruiser with the two-jillion-horsepower engine and we all took turns on water skis? Up and down the old lake at about a hundred miles an hour? Boy, instead of doing that, I wish we could have been in that good old rowboat, just rowing around, like Grandfather says."

"My father rowed very fast," this grandfather said, somewhat defensively. "Once he rowed so fast his straw hat fell off and floated away. We all laughed."

"Glorious," said one of the children. "What else did you do to kill—er, enjoy the day?"

"There were the fireworks, of course. We'd have a big sack—firecrackers and maybe two or three skyrockets. We'd save up our money and sometimes we'd have two or three dollars' worth."

"I guess the old Fourth isn't what it used to be," one of the little boys sighed. "The Merchants' Association is only going to have a two-and-a-half-hour fireworks show instead of three hours like they had last year."

119

"One year," this grandfather said, "we had two pinwheels."

"Last year," the more romantic of the girls sighed, "we had Farrah Faucett and Lee Majors all in fireworks, but this year all they're going to have is a reenactment of a spaceship blast-off."

"The fireworks weren't all," her grandfather said. "The high point of the whole day was when the Congressman made the speech."

"That sounds neat," cried the children. "Real heavy. What did you do, scream?"

"No, we just listened while he told us about the proud heritage of 1776."

"You didn't even picket?" asked the oldest boy. "Here was this speaker giving only one side of the question and you didn't picket or hand out pamphlets or sit down in the middle of the street?"

"No, we sat on folding chairs."

"And listened to the whole speech?"

"Yes," said this grandfather. "That was how the glorious Fourth used to be. Too bad you came along too late."

"It sounds glorious all right, Grandfather," said the kids, most of them keeping a straight face.

❖❖❖❖

Keeping Up with the Joneses' Gar-bagé

Anything that tears this country apart is to be regretted, of course, and one who feels this strongly cites the plastic trash sack as a divisive factor.

I will quote his letter, changing his wife's name from Edith to Ethel to protect his request for anonymity:

"Ethel and I have managed to cope with the fact that we

120

are a one-car family, but now as we look up and down the block on Monday mornings and we can see that everybody else can see that we have only one lonely plastic sack waiting to greet the trash man while more fortunate people have up to a dozen—well, we just hesitate to talk to the neighborhood children. Seems as you grow older the world imposes just one cruel blow after another."

Before going deeply into this matter I would like to make a comment or two. My correspondent signs himself "In Humility," which I very much doubt. He is a triple-distilled Scot, and I suspect that in his secret heart he is proud of having the fewest number of trash sacks on the block.

Also I hope he will excuse the expression "triple-distilled," since he does not drink, a fact which, by itself, cuts the amount of weekly trash fairly substantially.

Arguments and ad hominem aside, I think we are justified in examining the question of whether the number of trash bags determines status on the block. Let's assume that it does. After all, it makes sense in a country where the consumer is revered.

The efforts of elected officials as well as incorporated bands of Concerned Citizens are directed at preserving, safeguarding, and almost enshrining the consumer. The producer is left more or less to shift for himself and bad cess to him. So if the consumer is to be King of the Jungle it must follow that he who is to be mostly highly admired is he who consumes the most.

The one-bag family is as lightly regarded in the average neighborhood as the one-car family or the merely two-TV family. What would it avail a man if he could point to two boats and a camper in the backyard if all the combined efforts of his family could turn out was one plastic sack of trash?

It could be argued that before we had the plastic sacks we had the barrels, and it was just as humiliating to set out only

121

one barrel while others were lining the curb with four or five.

The answer is that with the barrels you could fake it. The barrels didn't have to be full. I will not mention names, but there were those who had false bottoms on their trash barrels, along the lines of the shot glasses in the less pleasant bars, permitting a very thin layer of debris to look like a barrel o'er-brimming.

It would be difficult to try a similar trick with plastic sacks.

A family might put out two half-filled sacks instead of one that was tightly packed. But they would immediately earn a reputation as poseurs. This sort of thing would rank along with riding around with your car windows up in the summertime to try to give the impression that you had air conditioning, while at the same time perspiration is dripping from the brow.

Better to be an open under-consumer than a clandestine one with social ambitions.

I may be mistaken, but it seems to me that there are more garage sales since the introduction of the plastic trash sacks. People who feel insecure of their place in the social hierarchy are going out and buying other people's junk for no other reason than to throw it away.

A simpler solution, and one which I think will recommend itself to my Scottish friend, is merely to slip out in the early dawn and tote a few of the neighbors' trash sacks over and put them in front of your house.

You will no longer be sneered at as a below-average consumer. Also, the friendly neighborhood burglar will put a check after your address, figuring that anybody who could afford to throw all that stuff away must have plenty more where it came from.

Have a Safe and Sane Summer

I know it is rather late in the season to come out with a series of hints on how to enjoy summer fun with a minimum of disastrous consequences, but quite a few days of heat and sun still remain.

With this in mind I will pass along some summertime suggestions which the standard instructions, put out by people like the Red Cross and the American Medical Association, tend to overlook:

Do not attempt to water-ski behind a canoe unless your wife and children are faster paddlers than the average for their age and weight.

If you wear a derby or almost any other kind of hat while swimming, the crawl is not a recommended stroke. Perhaps the best choice for your purpose is the breast stroke. This advice is also applicable if you are smoking a cigar. (N. B.: Many pools will not allow swimmers to smoke cigars in the pool. Check the printed regulations or ask the lifeguard.)

The middle-aged man who insists on playing softball should select whichever outfield position is under a shade tree. This not only is cooler but he need not worry about catching any fly balls as he can claim that he lost it in the tree.

When swinging out on a rope over a stream there is a precise moment at which it is a good idea to let go. It is hard to describe what that precise moment is, but if you miss it you will know.

For the beach picnic, suntan lotion and barbecue sauce should be kept in different shaped bottles unless it's a kind of strange group.

When a picnic is being organized, always be the first to volunteer to bring one item for the meal. This give you a chance to pre-empt the potato chips.

Remember insecticides can be harmful to your health. But

then so can insects. Life is made up of decisions.

Ladies in bikinis should not sit on metal chairs that have been left out in the sun.

Don't miss out on the wonderful thrills of surfing. Be sure you watch it on a color TV set.

When racing your child to the raft always be sure to let him or her win. That way somebody will be there to pull you up out of the water.

The disappearance of the handcranked phonograph has materially lessened the number of canoe upsets.

The ladies, bless them, have naturally fair and delicate skin. To make sure that your loved one will not suffer from painful sunburn, pick out a vacation spot where she will have to be in the kitchen for three meals a day plus washing the dishes. She will express her opinion of your thoughtfulness.

The theory that there is always a better picnic spot just around the next bend has some validity, but it can end up with you back at home eating on your own front stoop.

A tip to children having fun at the beach: When you have covered Daddy with sand, put up a stick or some sort of marker at the site so you can find him again, if necessary.

The number and length of the icicles painted on the "Air-Conditioned" sign are usually in inverse ratio to the coolness within.

Most snakes aren't poisonous, and those that are can't help it.

There are a number of remedies for poison ivy, none of which help much.

When children are hot and tired they will enjoy playing games in the car, such as seeing which one can drive Daddy crazy first.

Men past a certain age should wear lifejackets at all times while sitting on the dock or beside the pool. It's not a question of safety so much as it is that they look better with them on.

(The only thanks we expect for these tips is the knowledge

that we have done our small part in making your summer safe and enjoyable.)

❖❖❖❖

A Corny Problem

I have a brother I don't see much of, mainly because of the way he eats corn on the cob.

This is sort of hard to describe without hands, but what he did (and still does for all I know) was start in at the left end of the cob and eat all the way around it, then move to the right, revolve the cob again, and so on.

Most people, most normal people—people like me, in other words—operate on the typewriter principle. We eat along a row of kernels, or two or three rows according to mouth size, then we hear the tinkle of a mental bell, and we shift the carriage back from right to left and start all over again.

Am I being at all clear about this?

To use a military figure, most corn eaters I have ever encountered eat along the ranks. My brother devoured the cob by files.

Does calling what I think of as the normal method of corn eating the longitudinal approach and my brother's system the latitudinal attack help any?

The difference, to make it absolutely translucent, is between the lateral and the revolving method of eating corn on the cob.

My brother may have been the first time-motion study man. If he had applied his bright ideas to making automobiles instead of eating corn on the cob, he would be in a position to do a little something for his relatives today.

But all he would do was eat corn on the cob in that silly, unnatural way he had thought up and justify it by claiming it

125

was more efficient.

He said that the normal way of eating corn, the way Pocahontas taught Captain John Smith, the way George Washington would have eaten corn on the cob at Valley Forge if it hadn't been the dead of winter, was a waste of effort.

He said that using this silly system he thought up, you could keep your elbows planted on the table and eat a half, or anyway a third, of the ear just by twirling your fingers, and then you only had to make one simple little adjustment of your mouth and you had the next half (or third) all ready to eat.

He said that a lot of what was wrong with the country was that people were wasting their time with the old-fashioned typewriter method of eating corn.

I used to answer him with withering sarcasm, such as "It is a good thing that the man who invented the typewriter didn't eat corn on the cob the way you do or we'd still be writing with the goose quill pen."

It didn't bother him.

To be perfectly frank, the reason it bothered me was that I suspected he was probably right—logically and scientifically.

I couldn't match his arguments; all I had was faith, a deep inner conviction that, when it came to eating corn on the cob, I was right and he was wrong. The years have, I think, borne me out. In fact the victory for the straight-along-the-cob method of eating corn is so complete that I had been lulled into a sense of security.

Until the other night when I looked across the table at my little girl, who is, for the first time, showing a real interest in corn.

Do I have to tell you how she was eating it?

Once an odd bad strain gets into a family, it lasts for generations, as many a bald-headed, left-handed, blue-eyed fruit fly can testify. The sins of the uncles. . .

126

Used to Be the Vacation Column

The time rolls around when a man gets a little panicky and realizes that if he doesn't hurry on and write the vacation column it isn't going to get written. The problem is what kind to write.

Probably the easiest is the family vacation column where you make fun of your wife and kids and tell about hilarious breakdowns of the automobile and that sort of thing. The only trouble is that unless a man is an irresponsible sensation-monger he must write only the truth, and the truth is that I didn't take any trip with my family this summer, and if I had, the children, to say nothing of my wife, are mostly too old to do anything very funny.

Currently, the most popular vacation column is the one written by the deep-dish brains of Washington. It begins with a folksy and bucolic dateline, something like Pumpkin Hill, Md., or Forbes's Forge, Va., or Ned's Notch, N.H., and it goes like this:

"Here amid the August haze of the Rappanoodnick Mountains, with the sandpipers chirping in the furze and the wings of a Tufted Thrip making lazy circles in the sky, one gains a new perspective.

"In the rat race of the power struggle in Washington one tends to lose that perspective which one can only recapture under the conditions outlined above. Here, far from the frustrated ranting of hawks and doves one may concentrate instead upon the songs of [Note to Editor: Insert names of two birds. There's no dictionary up here].

"A man finds here a peace, a contentment, etc., etc.... "

Again honesty raises an obstacle. Most Washington oracles seem to own one of these rustic retreats where they can go and get away from the hustle and bustle and the constant banging away at the same old confusing issues—and give their readers a nice rest, too.

127

But I have no such spot in which to receive the benison of sylvan psychiatry.

This may be the year that the vacation column doesn't get written.

❖❖❖❖

Wife's Week Out

A man who pretends to write a column for a living is in pretty sad shape if he can't get a column out of his wife's being out of town for a week. There are all sorts of hilarious prospects—the tussle with the cooking, for example, the lack of clean shirts, the pots and pans piling up, and the cats going without food.

I mean when a man goes without uxorial companionship for an entire week, or even five days, you'd think he would be entitled to extract some lively copy out of it. Other men do it. I've read it, and it's good stuff, with telephone calls as to whether you want the man with the order to come on Tuesday or Wednesday, and being unable to cope because you don't know what they are talking about.

Well, I have just been through this experience, and none of this stuff happened. There were a few telephone calls, but they just said they'd call back. Obviously the callers felt that they didn't want to burden a busy man with these small matters.

After all, if you called U.S. Steel and got the president on the line you would prefer to try again with your small problem when some underling was available.

(A contrary thought intrudes: Maybe the callers didn't want to waste their time with a mere husband who obviously had no command of the situation.)

When wives go on their selfish little trips...no I don't mean that. When they go on a well-earned vacation...

Whatever, they tend to worry mainly about socks and shirts. There are instructions as to where the socks are and how they are to be washed should the need arise. There is a sign taped on the bathroom mirror: "Take Shirts to Laundry on Wed. Pick up Clean Ones. Love."

That word "Love" is on all the notes, whether it is about cleaning out the cats' pan or remembering trash pickup day. Wonderful people, women. They bring warmth to everything.

In my recent experience socks and shirts were no problem. True, I never did find the socks, but you wash out the same pair every night and they are ready in the morning. Some of us did not waste our time while in military service.

The shirts have been duly taken to the laundry. A laundry anyway. It may not be the right laundry because they did not have the clean ones. Or said they didn't anyway. But there is no real difficulty here.

New shirts may be purchased. That is they can if you know what size shirt you wear. Maybe you do. I don't. Still it's no problem if you are not embarrassed by loosening your tie in a crowded store so that a clerk can peek into your neckband.

I am a 16-33. I never knew that. I also never knew how much shirts cost. I thought they were about a buck, like they used to be, back when there was some sanity in the country.

There was no big deal about the cats. I fed them every day. I'm not too sure about their pan. I decided to let that go. I'm not on terms all that intimate with them.

Anyway, my wife will be surprised to see how well the cats look, except maybe the one that seems to have disappeared. She'll show up again, I think.

After all, a grown man can't stand at the back door and call, "Kitty, kitty," if he is going to maintain any sort of dignity in the neighborhood.

This kitchen stuff is no challenge either. What pots and pans? There is all kinds of stuff in the refrigerator if you rummage around and put it on a piece of bread. Then you eat it standing over the sink, and when you walk out of the kitchen it is as immaculate as when you entered, except for the towel where you wiped your hands.

Why do women make such an important project out of so simple a thing as a neat kitchen?

And what about this lonesomeness business? A wife will say, "Are you sure you won't be lonesome?"

No way. Not when I have my ball game on the radio and my Herodotus in the original whatever and my cats, or anyway the one I can find.

Also I cry quite a bit.

❖❖❖❖

The Art of Procrastination

The man who has it drummed into him as a youth that nothing should be put off until tomorrow that can be done today has to look out for bitterness when he grows up and discovers most of life's rewards going to the procrastinators.

Procrastination may be the thief of time, but it is the road to promotion.

The man who sees a job to be done and does it gets another job to do as a prize. Whereas the man who sees a job to be done and takes a month off to research the project and think through its ramifications is given a two-week vacation to recover from the experience.

If we may tune in on the conversation between two high-level tycoons at a costly luncheon we may hear Follansbee say to Clatchworthy:

"What do you think of young Fred Huckleberry in marketing?"

"Fine young man," Clatchworthy replies. "I gave him a bit

of work to do last week and had a call from him today from Bermuda. He is thinking the whole thing through in depth."

"Touching all the bases, eh?" says Follansbee, approvingly.

"Yes, reminds me of myself when young. The Founder once asked me to make a decision on the color of blotting paper in the board room. I immediately set sail for the south of France to check on the azure of the sky, the sand-color of the sand, and so on. I cabled him, of course, and he was tremendously impressed, upped my stipend."

"I can quite see why," says Follansbee. "I recall that it once took you three months to select the proper weight of paper clip for general office use. It caused quite a stir in the firm. You became known as a procrastinator's procrastinator."

"Thank you," says Clatchworthy. "That's why I am quite enthusiastic about young Huckleberry. He knows how to stall a job along. So few of his generation do, you know. It's almost a lost art."

"True, sadly true," says Follansbee. "We have a lad in the research department whom I asked for some data on a proposed packaging change. Had it on my desk the next morning."

"Shocking," says Clatchworthy.

From this bit of overheard conversation we may guess which young man has his foot firmly on the ladder of success. Certainly not the one who saw a job to be done and did it.

Young men must realize a few things. In the first place, the senior executive who has assigned the task has been putting off for six months the decision as to what sort of job to ask you to do.

Obviously, if you do it in a hurry he will have to think up something else for somebody to do, which is the last thing he wants.

Let us say that A is the top boss. After procrastinating for several weeks, he tells B, on the next lower echelon, to see about the Butterworth matter, whatever that may be. B fiddles with it for a few months, then passes it down to C, who is you.

The longer you refrain from doing anything about it, the happier everybody is. Once in a while A can ask B about it and B can say that C is working on it. Nothing is accomplished and yet everyone can assure everyone else that wheels are turning.

Any kind of quick action would throw off the timing of the entire organization, which is constructed along the lines of a fine Swiss watch.

There is also the pretty good chance that if everybody dallies along the way A will retire or old man Butterworth will die, either of which melancholy events will permit B and C (after suitable delays) to close the Butterworth matter without ever having done anything at all about it.

The man who jumps right in and gets things done may, as used to be said, make the fur fly, but he isn't likely to become a vice-president.

❖❖❖❖

No Joy in Mudville

We must, of course, hold to the hope that it won't happen, but the strike of the major league baseball players forced us to give thought to the unthinkable—a summer without baseball.

Tremendous problems of economics and sociology loom. The view from the boardrooms of peanut, popcorn, and hot dog corporations is dim. Mustard stocks are shaky.

There are always those who try to be facetious about serious matters. They point out that, without baseball, fewer office boys' grandmothers will have funerals during the season. The wheeze is outmoded. In the first place most games are played at night when office boys do not need excuses for being away from their posts. Secondly there are no more office boys; their rung on the ladder of success is now occupied by management trainees.

It would be doubly unfortunate if baseball were to be suspended during a year when a national election was being contested. Experience has taught that the best way to cool hot and rancorous political debate is to substitute an argument over whether the Skipper should or shouldn't have lifted the ace portsider in the seventh inning.

If not quite the opiate of the people, baseball is at least their tranquilizer, and while public tranquillity may not be the highest possible aim there is still a great deal to be said for it.

In previous campaign years there have been the televised games to offer some relief from the constant barrage of radiation from the candidates' teeth as they bring their charisma to bear upon us from the tube.

If it should come to that, couldn't last year's games be rerun on the teevy? I don't see anything wrong with that. Very few people watch from any real interest in how the game comes out. The main thing is that it gives a man a chance to get away from yard work and an excuse for telling the kids to pipe down for gosh sakes.

To make it even more pleasing entertainment, the video-tapes of two or even three different games might be spliced together, thus creating what would be, in effect, whole new ball games.

Also I would like to suggest that the stadiums might be kept open. This would enable the fans to engage in all the traditional side activities which make Our National Pastime what it is. There would be the traffic jams, the fender smashings, the consumption of the concessionaire's wares, the straggling through the stands, and the waving yoo-hoo to friends.

I see no reason why such occasions as cap day and halter top day and radio appreciation day shouldn't be held whether or not baseball is actually played.

Without the teams on the field, I should think that the price of tickets could be somewhat reduced.

The severest test would be when the World Series dates come along, just as the need for some shelter from the political storm is most keenly felt.

It is the time when the cartoonists show Gus Fan looking up at the sky where a glorious sun, with stitched seams like a baseball, is shown driving away gloomy clouds labeled "Everyday Problems." I have never been sure how accurate a representation of the public mind that cartoon is, but I would hate to see a great tradition die.

In all fairness it must be said that there are some people who are sicker of baseball by the end of the summer than they are of politics. Perhaps a year without baseball would provide an opportunity to measure just how widespread that attitude is.

We must fight off the dark and un-American whisperings that there might be a chance, if baseball went away, that nobody would miss it.

❖❖❖❖

Oh, Fudge!

There is something pejorative (a word I am forced to use once a month in order to hold the franchise) about the word fudge. Something described as fudge is assumed to be of little weight and value in the world.

But have we ever stopped to think of the role of fudge in our society? Has a definitive study been funded?

It is my admittedly unscientific guess that more good causes have been aided by fudge than by all the solemn do-good conclaves of our time. Fudge has saved churches from bankruptcy, sent high school bands to state tournaments, paid off mortgages for senior citizens, kept day nurseries alive, sustained culture, bought baseball uniforms, and financed roadside beautifications.

When any worthy project feels the pinch of economic reality, the board of directors sits around and says, ahem, well yes, there is always the prospect of federal assistance or perhaps the involvement of state and local units and the business community.

Then some particularly profound thinker removes his pipe from his mouth and says, "Fudge."

To which others reply, "Of course. Why didn't we think of that? The very thing. Fudge, to be sure."

So the board members go home and tell the auxiliary, meaning their wives, that it is going to be fudge again and the auxiliary sighs, "Good grief," and starts building up the fire under the fudge kettle.

One reason men on philanthropic boards like fudge as a money-raising event is that it pretty well leaves them out. The lady folk do the cooking and the kid-persons form the sales force.

Firmly established in the American pantheon is Mom's apple pie. I am not going to put the knock on it, but it is my belief that fudge has done more for this country than apple pie ever thought of doing.

Plus the fact that there is such a thing as bad apple pie, some of it cooked by Moms. Bad fudge is almost impossible. Not that some fudge isn't worse than others, but the basic operation of fudge-manufacture is so simple that it is difficult to go very far wrong.

Even men, if they wanted to, could make fudge. In fact, I know some who do and are not thought of as unmanly for the accomplishment.

Whole generations of nondelinquents of both sexes were reared by being turned loose in the kitchen to make fudge while Mom lay down with a cool cloth on her forehead.

I may have told you about the time when I was a tyke and was being baby-sat by an uncle who was very little older. He made us some great fudge, with the exception of the fact that it turned out white. The reason was that my grandmother kept the silver polish in the can marked "Cocoa," so I always figured he was in the clear, although my mother and grandmother viewed the matter otherwise.

They wouldn't let me eat any of it, although my uncle snuck a few pieces and said it was the best silver polish fudge he had ever eaten. This was before all the hoorah about truth in labeling.

Anyway, there was a time in this country when every American above the age of seven knew how to make fudge. Who is to say it was not a happier time, disregarding the odd war or depression?

Now, I suppose that even a lot of the fudge sold for fund-raising purposes is machine made, instead of being the product of the auxiliary's loving hands. I count this a loss, but it does not detract from the major part played by fudge in the welfare of this great nation of ours.

Ask where we would be without fudge, and I will answer, "Where are we now?"

Fudge is a versatile comestible. You can make it, sell it, even eat it. And, if desperate enough, pad out a column about it.

Friends of the Jellyfish

The House of Representatives has extended the program to provide for "control or elimination" of jellyfish in coastal waters. Nobody asked me about this. And nobody asked you. How does the government know that we want the jellyfish eliminated, or even controlled?

Not being a coastal person I have never seen a jellyfish, so I am completely unprejudiced in the matter. Unprejudiced, some will say, and also uninformed. But let it be remembered that I have been crusading for years to save the Great Whooping Crane, and I never saw one of them either. I wouldn't know a Great Whooping Crane if it walked up and pecked me in the eye, which it might well do, gratitude being what it is among feathered folk.

I am dubious about these distinctions in conservation. If we go all out to save the crane, shouldn't we do the same for the jellyfish?

As a civil libertarian I feel that everybody is entitled to the same protection by the law, no matter how we may abhor their character and opinions. The Great Whooping Crane is, off its pictures anyway, a lovely, graceful creature, winging its patterns against a gibbous moon.

The jellyfish, at least in its photographs, leaves a great deal to be desired.

Do we really feel that only the beautiful species of the world should be preserved? If this is the case, a great number of us are in serious difficulty.

The jellyfish, I am informed, is a nuisance on the beach, nipping the bather on the big toe or worse. Look at it from the jellyfish's point of view. He was there first, before they even built the bathhouse or opened the first pizzeria on the boardwalk.

It's hard to worry about people on beaches anyway. What are they doing? Why aren't they working somewhere? If they want to get wet why don't they jump into a swimming pool, run through a lawn sprinkler, or open a fire hydrant the way nature intended?

A more serious point is that we shouldn't pick out the animals, vertebrate or otherwise (it's their own business) that we plan to preserve merely on the basis of their lovability. Apparently we are now winning the battle to save the alligator. I applaud, although I have never met an alligator I liked, especially including the one that once lived in our spare bathtub. It really wasn't a spare, but it quickly became one as soon as the alligator moved in.

I have never had a jellyfish in the bathtub and don't intend to, except that I might if it would save an endangered species from elimination.

Probably what disturbs me most about the prospect of the full power of the government being unleashed upon the jellyfish is that it is such a defenseless creature. Or at least it sounds that way.

For years it has been the synonym for weakness. It has, as I understand it, no backbone and very little interest in obtaining one. The fact that it stings bathers is not contradictory. A lot of weak people have their small viciousnesses.

We are being asked to safeguard the Great Whooping Crane, the Grizzly Bear, the Bald Eagle, all of whom have grand and impressive names. The jellyfish has no panache. Even when it upgrades itself into a Portuguese Man o' War it is still a jellyfish at heart, or whatever.

The times cry aloud for a Friends of the Jellyfish League, with a paid secretary and annual meetings. In fifteen minutes of study I can't find a single redeeming quality about the jellyfish.

Anything so completely useless is worth defending. Annual dues of about fifty dollars a year sound right. More details later.

❖❖❖❖

Store It!

Those of us who occasionally browse through *Pad & Lot* or some others of what are known in the magazine business as shelter books quickly become aware of one overriding concern of America. Or at least of that section of America which meets the demographic standards of these periodicals which appeal to the man (or possibly woman) with a desire to decorate the living room or grow something herbaceous in the yard.

The magic word is: Storage.

No magazine in this field appears without devoting the bulk of its pages (or so it seems, anyway) to figuring out clever ways to add shelves, cabinets, and drawers to unsuspecting nooks.

Apparently Americans have enough stuff. What they need are places to put it in.

I assume it is a middle-class problem. The poor don't have the belongings. The rich may have more things than anybody else but they can buy two or three additional houses to put them in. Or they can keep on getting divorces and dividing things up.

In between are the in-between people who are always, well, in between.

They are the ones who seem to be obsessed by the idea that they need more room to contain their possessions. It would, of course, be un-American (and possibly antihuman) to suggest that what they really need are fewer possessions.

So the first thing the home handyman is expected to make is a box. The box is used to contain the tools which he used to make the box.

He is now ready to expand his empire. He may, however, make a few side forays first. His next construction may be a box for birds. People who want everything neatly tucked away inside their homes don't want their birds flying around at random. So they box the birds. Of course, they call it a birdhouse and provide a hole for the bird to go in and out of.

That last statement (about the hole in the birdhouse) recalls a friend of mine who built the customary box for his tools, the saw, hammer and so on. Then he nailed the lid firmly down.

I asked him what he did with the hammer he had used to nail the lid on, and he said he gave it back to the neighbor from whom he had borrowed it. He then retired from the building of storage facilities and spent the rest of his life watching TV.

"The main attraction of television to the modern American," he explained, "is that it comes in a box. There is no need to build anything to store it in."

But he is an exception. Most men make the mistake of hinging the lid on that first box so that they can get the tools out and build ever more elaborate boxes.

Only by this time, the boxes are piled on top of one another and become either wall systems or room dividers. The difference is that the wall system is a bunch of boxes against a wall, while the room divider juts out into the room, and therefore has to be painted on both sides.

Other good things to do are to build boxes under beds, over doorways, up staircases and on top of the refrigerator. The theory, one supposes, is that eventually there is a place for everything to be shelved, binned, or drawered. However, as is well known, Nature abhors an empty box, and every storage container automatically fills up the minute it is constructed. The man who begins to build boxes, shelves, and cabinets will keep on adding to them the rest of his life, unless he joins some abstruse sect and retires to the high Himalayas.

And it's probably just as well that there is no end to the storage problem. Because if a family ever reached the point where everything was neatly tucked away, why what would be left in life? Or life according to the Lovely Living magazines.

AUGUST

Water-skiing

There are some of us who, when we appear on beach or dock, give the impression of being high school athletes who have gone to seed. Others of us look like seedy high school kids who have gotten worse.

In either case there is very little chance of our learning how to water-ski. And yet the man who does not water-ski does not fit in with current life-styles. He is Odd Man Out. He may be passed over for promotion.

Invited to the boss's summer cottage where water-skiing is to be the big event he will cut a ridiculous figure. The word in the board room on Monday will be that a man who cuts that ridiculous a figure cannot be trusted with any other figures, especially those involving profits and losses.

I do not know exactly when this craze for water-skiing began. It must have come up when I was out of town. At least I wasn't aware of it until it had become full-blown and there was no possibility of my ever catching up with it.

The *Encyclopaedia Britannica* which I carry with me at all times (the paperback edition) says that it all started in France in the 1920s. True, it does seem the sort of thing that might appeal to a people who are traditionally fond of light wines and dancing. My own guess, however, is that it was inspired by the Germans as a form of retaliation for the harsher sections of the Treaty of Versailles.

The encyclopedia further informs me that "in this sport the thrill of speed can be savoured without the usually accompanying danger."

That, of course, is easily said, especially by someone who can get away with an added touch of class by spelling it "savoured."

In my case it involves the thrill of standing waist deep in water while savoring the thrill of being laughed at by small children and worse.

It is a pretty good rule for living never to participate in any sort of activity that seems to come naturally to scrawny kids, blue-haired ladies, or fat men smoking cigars. All of these classes and many, many more seem to be proficient in water skiing. They may be seen out there savoring on Lake Watchanabee from morn till night.

They will advise the non-skier that there is nothing to it, which may be true, but whatever that nothing is, it is a nothing that I don't seem to have. The water ski and I do not have a viable relationship.

I can't explain it. Some people can water-ski. Others have other qualities, which is probably true of me although I cannot think what they might be.

The politician who does not water-ski might as well forget about entering the presidential primaries, except possibly in New Hampshire.

So it is important that a man water-ski. For a while I tried arguing against the idea. I said that a man could be a dedicated employee, a grand husband, outstanding father, and loyal patriot without indulging in a foreign aberration of this type.

I made up lists of great Americans who did not water-ski.

Many of them crossed large bodies of water but they always stayed in the boat, usually with someone else rowing.

This did no good, of course. Men are measured in our society by whether or not they water-ski.

The only answer is to develop techniques for appearing to water-ski without actually getting out there and making a fool of yourself. One good way is to suggest that you have been skiing all morning and that now it is time for the others to have a go at it. If the others fall off the skis it helps build your own status to laugh loudly and shake your head in wonderment that anyone could be so clumsy.

Do not make the mistake of pleading that you forgot your swim togs. There are always friends who will lend you some.

My best success has been in explaining that I do not savor domestic skis and can only use the ones I have personally imported for me from France.

But in all honesty none of these things works forever. Eventually the word gets around that you're the fellow who doesn't water-ski, and you have to sit in the rear of the dune buggy.

❖❖❖❖

The Courtship, Spawning Habits, and Migratory Patterns of the Common Coat Hanger

As a matter of fact, very little is known about this subject, and a lot of what people think they know is merely folklore.

It has been generally assumed, for example, that coat hangers breed in dark closets. The reasons for this assumption are obvious. If you clean out all the coat hangers except two, you will find after returning home from a brief vacation that there are as many hangers in there as ever, and probably more. This indicates that something is going on.

A housewife in Tenafly, N.J., reports that she left only one coat hanger in the front hall closet, went to spend two weeks with her sister in Terre Haute, and when she came back there were 63 hangers. If we rule out parthenogenesis, which is virtually unknown in Tenafly, where did they all come from?

Some interesting research into this matter was done by a professor at Tufts College who left a wooden coat hanger and a wire coat hanger in a closet in his upstairs front bedroom. When he checked them a week later, there were fifty-seven, but all, except for the original wooden model, were wire coat hangers. Obviously there had been no crossbreeding or the Mendelian law would have been in operation and you would have had some wooden ones, some wire ones and some combinations, which is the way it works with blue eyes, brown eyes, and fruit flies, as everybody knows.

Fascinated by the problem, the professor took the two original hangers to his office and hung them in a closet, which he then locked. After forty-eight hours he unlocked the closet and they were both gone.

This illustrates a principle which can be most simply stated thus:

"Coat hangers disappear from places of employment in direct ratio to their multiplication in the home."

Like other postulates of pure science, this one has a practical application. Many a husband has heard his wife utter as follows: "Oh, what shall we do with all the coat hangers?"

All too often he merely answers, "What's for dinner?"

But if he wishes to be helpful he offers to take an armload of them to the office. Within a week they will all be gone. Conversely, the closets at home will be as full as ever.

Is there a strong homing instinct in these little devices? If some generous foundation would care to come up with a grant, I might try taking a flock of hangers to the office, banding them with serial numbers, and seeing if the same ones then reappear in the closet back home.

My guess is that they would not. Just as a working hypothesis, it seems to me that coat hangers do not "home" in the sense of returning to any particular base. But there is no doubt that they find the atmosphere of a residence more congenial than they do that of a place of business.

Nor do coat hangers care much for hotel rooms. Look into any closet in your home and you will find hangers from the Antlers Hotel in Colorado Springs; the Connor in Joplin, Missouri; the Bellevue-Stratford in Philadelphia; the Istanbul-Hilton; places you have never been in your life. How do they get there? Nobody knows.

Why doesn't science quit wasting time on outer space and look into this matter?

❖❖❖❖

Then They'll Be Sorry. . .

So many people worry about what to do with the retirement years that often desperate suggestions come up, such as sawing bottles into glasses or making birdhouses. I can only marvel at folk who feel this way. In my own case I have a number of things in mind which will keep me busy throughout the sunset years and, in fact, until about midnight.

There may be scoffers in the audience who think that I am now going to lie a lot about taking up the study of Greek and/or the ophicleide. Something of the sort is farthest from my intent.

I have, as I think my friends will testify, spent years in building up a reputation as a nonhobbyist. The stamp will, by me, go uncollected, the shy warbler unobserved.

What I want to let you know, however, is that I am not without plans.

145

For one thing, I plan to answer radio station editorials, the ones that (presumably under some sort of gun from the Federal Communications Commission) say that responsible persons are invited to offer a differing opinion.

The trouble is that a man in the full flush of qualifying for a paycheck and paying off the mortgage seldom finds time to sit down and write a differing opinion to the editorialist at KWAK.

How often I have heard this editorial voice tell me that safe driving is a good thing, while suggesting that it would be perfectly willing to listen if I didn't agree. I have been tempted to write, pointing out that the great civilizations of the world have been known for their crummy records in traffic safety.

"Dear KWAK," I have often felt like writing, "it is all very well to talk of traffic safety, but a careful reading of history will reveal that Rome declined and fell when they started putting safety belts in the chariots. This country was not built by safe drivers. So watch the Commie propaganda. Remember young, impressionable ears are listening."

It seems to me a satisfying senior citizenship could be built by disagreeing with these outrageous statements in favor of clean water, better (but cheaper) schools, lifejackets in the rowboat, better bus service, courtesy on the sidewalk, and nonlittering.

How unfortunate it is that we have to pass up the opportunity to come to grips with these controversial matters because we are still occupied with day-to-day concerns.

It is amazing how many men and women are willing to waste their final years of glorious freedom by trudging through museums or trying to catch fish. Many of these hours of release which will be mine someday will be spent in fighting City Hall, the Statehouse and the citadels of power in Washington.

In my lifetime I have paid X number of traffic tickets. In

146

all these incidents I have been 100 percent right and the police (bless and support them though I do) have been wrong. But I have always pleaded guilty. I have not unto mine own self been true. I have lacked the time to pursue these cases until the final rendering of judgment. I have taken the cowardly way out, as recommended in the old vaudeville routine, and paid the two dollars. But not when retirement lays upon me its benison of nothing else to do.

I shall fight traffic tickets, real estate assessments, and the rulings of the Internal Revenue Service. It will matter not if I win or lose; I will at last have had time to play the game.

I will read all those labels which urge the puzzled consumer to write for a full explanation of the ingredients, and I will write and get that explanation. I will read the owners' manuals for all the major appliances I have bought over the years. Heretofore I have had to quit without getting past "Hi there, I am your new electric toothbrush." Just too busy.

If I buy a new garment I will drop a line to Inspector No. 37 and tell him (or her) that he (or she) did a wonderful job (or not). I've always wanted to do this. If they're nice enough to give me their number, they deserve a personal line.

When then, those of you who are growing old along with me, do you fear inactivity? There is so much just lying around waiting to be done.

❖❖❖❖

Bulling with the Bullish

These are tough times to be a non-capitalist. I'm not talking about communism. Whether it is a tough time to be a Communist I couldn't say. What I mean is that the man who doesn't own a share of stock feels out of it.

It is the loneliest experience I have been through since the days when everybody was talking about quitting smoking cigarettes and I couldn't because I never had smoked cigarettes.

There are embarrassing moments. A newly met acquaintance, by way of getting the conversation in motion, says, "What's the market doing today?

I answer, "I think sweet corn is ten ears for seventy-nine cents."

The acquaintance moves restlessly, "I'm not in commodities myself. What's on the big board?"

"Well," I say, "They chalk it up there every noon. From here it looks like tuna delight and barbecued cheeseburgers."

"Never mind that," he says. "I understand that Affiliated Biodegradables has split."

"Split?" I ask. "You mean it has left town?"

After a little of this, he becomes a former acquaintance. There is no way for a man who is not involved in the market to hold up his end of a conversation.

As far as I know, when a woman tugs at her girdle it is a technical adjustment. Apparently there is another meaning on Wall Street.

Everybody assumes you are in the market. You are asked how you are. You say you are fine. The interrogator says you can't be fine with the Dow at 600 or some such figure.

A a desperate effort to pretend that you know what he is talking about, you say, "My Dow is not 600. Last time I went to the doctor it was 52 over 168."

It seldom works because I know as little about blood pressure as I do about stocks and couldn't say whether 52 over 168 is even a reasonable guess. Experience has taught me that people who know what the Dow-Jones average is also know their blood pressure and, more than likely, their pulse rate.

Nor is there any relief to be found by fleeing the clouds of cigar smoke. Among the ladies you find the same expertise on the fluctuations of stocks.

There was a time when you could talk to women about how much frizz was to be in the hairdo next year and where the peplum was to be situated or what was the newest in formulas for the baby. Now there is no interest in those matters.

"We have gotten out of glamour stocks and into blue chips," a matron will announce.

"Glamour Stocks and Blue Chips?" you ask. "Boy, they sure come up with some wild names for these new subdivisions. But as long as you like the neighbors and the schools are good, what difference does it make?"

I had one rather wild experience with a lady who asked me my opinion of mutual funds. And you won't believe this but I thought she said mutual fun and muttered something about I suppose it was all right with consenting adults before I retreated to the other end of the room.

Please understand that I am not proud of my nonparticipation in this facet of American life. One must, after all, be involved. It's just that all my life I have invested my money in steaks and baby shoes and sofas and gasoline and other things which never seemed to leave any money over to set me up as the Boy Plunger of Wall Street.

I guess it has been unpatriotic of me, and it is embarrassing when times like these come along.

What I may do is buy a share of stock, one that expert advisers will tell me is a real dog. Then, when I sell at 30 points lower, I can, for the rest of my life, lament that I was wiped out in '70.

At least I would be more honest than my Uncle Ed who always explained he was wiped out in '29. He didn't own even one share.

❖❖❖❖

The Secret to Success

The other day I asked a man whom I had always admired for his equanimity and unfailing good humor to what he attributed these accomplishments.

"Young man," he said (his eyesight is not too good), "years ago I adopted a great principle not only to govern my life but to simplify it. Briefly, it is: Never do for fun what another man does for a living."

"How does that help?" I asked.

"Well," he said, "in the first place it keeps me from doing a lot of things around the house that I might otherwise get involved in. For example, nothing is more fun than carpentry, watching the wood shavings fall around the hunk of wood you are planing into a breadboard or a handy storage cabinet for your helpmeet.

"But there are carpenters who plane and nail and saw for a living. It demeans them if amateurs pretend that they can do the same work.

"Nor do I deliver sermons to my friends, although it is a tempting and widely practiced hobby. This is the job for the clergy. Nor do I practice medicine for the enjoyment of the thing, diagnosing symptoms over the poker table, for example. In fact, I think I'll give up poker, much as I love it, because I understand there are people who support their families by this sort of endeavor.

"Just as I leave medicine to the doctors, I leave legal advice to the lawyers. I refuse to tell anybody when to sue or how to plead, although many people seem to find this a rewarding hobby.

"I do not fish for the same reason. What right do I have to make light of dredging the finny folk from lake or stream when there are others who depend on it for a livelihood? I let farmers do the farming, denying myself the indisputable pleasure of raising tomatoes or zucchini squash.

"When tempted to set foot upon a golf course I consider that if I were to make a game out of golf it would reflect on the lifetime career of Nicklaus, Palmer, Watson, *et al*.

"Sitting outdoors painting a sylvan scene would undoubtedly be relaxing, but the pleasure would be spoiled for me knowing that all over the world there were professional artists who would give anything in the world to get a day off from the easel, so I let those who depend on art to feed their families do all the painting."

"That doesn't leave much does it?" I asked.

"Oh," he said, "I forgot to mention that I also do not whip up tasty meals in the kitchen, that being the job of a chef. Some men even make a hobby of baking bread, which is an insult to the professional dignity of bakers. The same goes for cutting my own hair, an assignment properly belonging to the tonsorial brotherhood.

"But to answer your question, there is still quite a bit left. I can read or go to the movies or watch television. Now I know there are critics who make a living doing those things, but they are so small in number as not to be statistically significant. I take walks, which nobody else does professionally, except mailmen, but that's different because they carry a mailbag, which I never do."

"And that," I asked, "is the secret of your equanimity?"

"Pretty much so," he replied.

"Also," I said, "it sounds as though you are pretty lazy."

"Yes," he smiled calmly. "That helps, too."

❖❖❖❖

Last of the Pioneers

After thirty years or so of marriage my wife felt she knew me well enough to venture a personal question.

"Why is it," she said, "that whenever you stop at a full-service gasoline station you get out of the car?"

"Well," I began, "there are times. . . ."

"I am not talking about that," she said, "or buying a candy bar. You just get out and stand beside the car. Even if the sun is broiling down or if it's raining or snowing. You get out of the car. All you have to do is roll the window down a few inches and sign the slip. That's the way they do it in the commercials."

"Not Joe Namath and George Gobel," I pointed out. "They get out of the car."

"That's so they can get in the camera shot with the gasoline pumps," she said. "Nobody is taking your picture. And Joe Namath and George Gobel or whomever don't get out when it's raining or snowing."

"I don't stand out in the rain or snow," I said defensively. "I go in the office and look at the battery displays."

"Yes," she said, "but why? I've always wondered. I've asked my friends and their husbands never get out of the car."

I said that was a mighty small thing to complain about, and she said she wasn't complaining, merely asking a question.

And I must admit it is a good question. I don't know why I get out of the car. Or rather I guess I do but it's not a very good reason. I get out of the car because my father always got out of the car.

I grew up thinking that it was a sign of maturity to get out of the car at filling stations. Children and wives stayed in the car unless there was some pressing reason for them to get out.

This country was built by men who get out of the car at filling stations. They were the descendants of the pioneers who jumped off the front seat of the Conestoga wagon to water the oxen, while the women and children huddled in the rear.

My father knew, if possible, less about automobiles than I

152

do, but he must have made a powerful impression on me, getting out of the car and dealing with the filling station proprietor as he did. I suppose what it really got down to was that my father thought getting out of the car was the Thing to Do. And I learned from his example, which is why I do it.

Since my wife brought the subject up I have taken an informal and unscientific poll which leads me to believe that I may be the only man left in America who gets out of his car at full-service filling stations. It gives a man a lonesome feeling, sort of like being the last ivory-billed woodpecker in the Big Piney or wherever he lives.

Some men have said that sometimes they get out of the car and sometimes they don't. What kind of people are these? That's sort of like saying sometimes you tuck your napkin under your chin and sometimes you leave it in your lap. (And I must say the slipshod method of leaving the napkin in the lap also is gaining in popularity.)

No. It is either correct to get out of the car or it isn't, and let us not shilly-shally about it.

Besides if you stay in the car you can't kick the tires.

❖❖❖❖

So Long, Farewell, Auf Wiedersehen, Good-bye

About the best thing summer does is come to an end. I don't mean that I am glad to see it depart. The thing is that it goes out of business with decisiveness. There is no dragging of feet, no temporizing, no waffling.

Labor Day is it. The portcullis comes down with a clang. The calendar may insist that summer is going to be around for three more weeks, or something equally ridiculous. The heat may linger, but summer knows as well as the rest of us that it's been here and gone.

It is a quality we admire in people. As you winnow out your roster of friends over the years you discover that the ones worth having are those who, at some time during the evening—and it gets earlier with the years—stand up and say, "We're leaving." And they do.

There is none of this lingering at the doorstep with the door open, allowing the air-conditioning as well as the cat to escape. They get up, put on their hats or whatever, and that's that. They are also in the great tradition of summer when they are playing host. In this case, they get up and say, "You are leaving."

Summer does the same thing. It tells us it is leaving and so are we, even though we might like to hang around a little longer.

There are some who get their feelings hurt by this abruptness. Summer prefers to be surgical about it.

As is said to be the case with a love affair, the clean break is best.

On the Tuesday after Labor Day you wake up and find it's all over. No need hanging around the telephone waiting for summer to call and say that it was all a silly mistake and how about having lunch together. There may be some pain, but it is soon forgotten. Isn't that much better?

Other seasons will drag on, dangling you on a string, pretending to be gone one day and back the next. Summer says what it means and what it means is that it is leaving on Labor Day; drain the pool, deflate the beach ball, pack the kids off to school, and don't bother to write.

Perhaps I appreciate summer's decisiveness even more in an election year when all about us is compromise and on-the-other-handedness. When candidates are backing away from what they said in the primaries or at the conventions and redefine for us what it was they really meant, it is a pleasant relief to find some element in our life which doesn't quibble.

When summer took over on Memorial Day it was with the

promise that it would depart on Labor Day. And this is the promise it invariably keeps.

Summer is like the proud man who, when the time comes to retire, cleans out his desk and leaves. Summer doesn't ask to be kept on as a consultant. It doesn't hang around, looking over the shoulders of the other seasons. It puts all its belongings in a cardboard box and catches the bus.

It refuses to copy the aging athlete trying to squeak through for just enough longer to earn a pension. There are no garrulous recitations of past triumphs.

When it is time to go, it goes. Maybe that is the most important lesson summer has to tell us.

It doesn't even give us a parting wave. It is like the wise visitor who says, "Don't bother driving me to the airport. I'll catch a cab."

And that's class.

SEPTEMBER

All Torn Up

Only a few brief months ago, or so it seems, we started having a modest amount of papering, painting, plastering, and so on done at our house. The motivating forces behind this enterprise assured me that the rearrangement of my lifestyle would be minimal during the process.

There were public relations efforts, such as signs saying, "Paint We Must" and "Your Dollars at Work."

They weren't needed. It is true that the suggestion that the daily routine would not be disturbed turned out to be false. But it was all for the best.

Life, I have discovered, in a home that is, in the words of the Keeper of the Flame, "all torn up," is much more comfortable than when everything is in order.

It is hard to count the ways, but for example, I have not answered a letter since mid-July, I assume that the mail arrives, but then it disappears in the melange of brushes, caulking guns, paint buckets, tarpaulins, and wallpaper samples that comprise the decor of my place of residence. So I am relieved of any worry about whether the outside world is trying to communicate with me and is expecting a reply.

If there is anybody to whom I owe money, I haven't seen the bills and couldn't find my checkbook in any event.

All the furniture, you understand, is in the middle of the rooms, covered with plastic drop cloths. In some drawer of some cabinet pushed up against some other cumbersome and, as far as I know, immovable household fixture is the bottle of pills I am supposed to take three of a day. I can't find them and have never felt better.

Newspapers are thrown on the floor, giving every day that delightfully relaxed Sunday morning feeling. There are three books that I absolutely must read because they were written by friends who wanted my reaction, or said they did. There is no possible way for me to find them, so I am absolved of any guilt feeling about not having read them.

No time is wasted in dusting anything, straightening anything, polishing anything or putting anything away. To do so would be like adjusting the linen napkins in the Grand Salon while the ship is sinking.

Every member of the family is entitled to a place to sleep and one chair. The bathroom is kept clear. A sort of jungle trail leads to the icebox and the stove, but cooking is mainly stuff that can be heated in its own foil. Every denizen has a cup, plate, and choice of fork or spoon. That's it.

Meals are enjoyed under the dining-room table. When carefully lifted, the tarpaulin will reveal a corner of the television screen. In this manner the family can share a primitive communal closeness which is so often lacking in the depersonalized world of today.

Entertaining is, of course, out of the question. It is very helpful this time of year to be able to say: "Why, of course, we were thinking of giving a sit-down orgy for 75 of our dearest friends, including you and Melville, but it is out of the question, what with the house being torn up and all."

Friends will murmur (or mutter) that they understand.

Door-to-door sales personnel are easily discouraged. They

take one look at the shrouded forms of what may be tables and chairs, but could be something infinitely worse, and edge their way back out the door.

The work at our house is proceeding with skill and dispatch. But for the reasons cited above, and others, I will hate to see it come to an end.

The home that's undergoing redecoration may be a bit untidy but it's certainly snug.

I dread the day when things get straightened around again so that we can find the telephone and feel compelled to answer it.

Walking Room Only

With football in its present state of high popularity, the problem, admittedly a pleasant one from a financial standpoint, arises of how to get more persons into a sold-out stadium.

If you have 60,000 seats you can accommodate only 60,000 fans, plus perhaps a few more if there is some standing room.

My plan, which I offer free to professional front offices or university athletic directors, is to sell walking tickets. It has been my observation that at all sports spectacles there is a group, numbering perhaps in the thousands, who do nothing during the contest but walk back and forth in the aisles and up and down the steps.

I have never been sure why they want to come to the game, but apparently just strolling about the stadium, presumably listening to the announcements and the cheers, is their idea of a big time.

It must be admitted that stadium walkers get more exercise

than the sitters or the standers (or those who alternately sit and stand).

I have no intention of criticizing these fans. In fact there is something admirable about a man or woman who will battle the traffic and the parking to walk from Section 12 to Section 46 and back again for three hours.

The point I wish to make, however, is that these walkers have to buy seats to get into the park even though they have no intention of sitting in them. This strikes me as unfair on two counts: First it is unfair to the walker who has to pay for a seat he doesn't want. Second, it deprives someone else of a chance to buy that seat.

My proposal is that these people be permitted to pay a reduced price for a walking ticket. Then the seats they formerly had bought could be sold to additional fans who hitherto had been unable to get in.

The walking ticket would be in the form of a tag worn in the lapel so ushers could recognize the walkers and make sure that they keep walking.

They would, of course, be allowed to stand briefly in front of the concession stands. In my experience the walkers are great consumers of hot dogs, peanuts, and other traditional goodies. All that roaming about the stadium apparently does wonders for the appetite.

I don't see how this plan could help but greatly increase the number of people who can be accommodated at sports spectacles.

There may be those who will argue that there really isn't a group of people who do nothing but walk around in the stadium—that, instead, everybody does a certain amount of it.

I don't think there is much to be said for this point of view. Granted most people do some walking at the game. (Inevitably everybody has to walk to his seat and eventually away from it.)

But if you are seated where you can get a good view of the pedestrian traffic you soon will discover that the same faces keep recurring. These are the true, the dedicated walkers and they are the ones I have in mind in my surefire plan.

Wake up, sports moguls.

❖❖❖❖

Autumn—a Communist Plot

Congressman Sludgepump rises and is recognized.

Mr. Speaker:

I am sending to the clerk a copy of a bill which I have marked HR: 16897. It has for its purpose the regulation of the costly, wasteful, and generally unsatisfactory coloration of the leaves in the autumn, or fall as it is known in some parts of the nation.

For many years I have been concerned about this undisciplined affair which, for a few weeks, makes a garish display upon the hillsides of our country with little regard to the needs, or indeed the wishes, of the farmer, housewife, and small businessman.

I would like to read a letter from an eleven-year-old constituent, Miss Susy Belle Sausage, who writes me as follows:

"Last week my father was driving us in the country. My mother was along and my Aunt Delphine and my brother, Ned, but you can forget about him.

"Just as we were going around a curve on highway No. 50 my mother and my Aunt Delphine screeched look at the beautiful maple or maybe it was a oak. Anyway, my father thought there was a bee loose in the car or somebody had dropped a cigarette on the upholstery when he heard the yelling and he screeched on the brakes and the car swerveled around and might have hit this big truck coming the other way if it hadn't been for my father's razor-sharp reflexes as he is fond of describing them.

"He says that all this color in the trees is a menace to traffic safety especially if there are screechable females in the car.

"I asked him if it was such a danger why didn't somebody do something about it, and he said that is a good idea and somebody ought to write to our Congressman and I said who is that and he said he didn't know, but I looked him up and he is you.

"So won't you please make a law that there shall be no more red, yellow, or worse trees, especially on curves? It will save the lives of many little girls and their families and even their brothers, if you think that is important.

"Sincerely, Susy Belle Sausage, age 11."

I wish to say to honorable members on both sides of the aisle that this is a human document which should not be lightly disregarded. Safety on our highways has always been one of my primary concerns, as it has been of many other distinguished and able members.

There are other considerations as well. The autumnal foliage stimulates many otherwise nontroublesome citizens to the practice of poetry. In these days of crisis at home and abroad, it is an economic and social waste to have poetry widespread in the land.

The Russians and the Red Chinese, I am convinced, do not indulge themselves in this manner. Does a poem on the beauties of the sumac and the sassafras marching across the landscape like an army with crimson banners help us find more oil? I think not.

Have you ever asked yourself this question: "If I were a Communist, what would I do to bring the great and powerful United States to its collective knees?"

If you have asked yourself this question, I am sure you have answered yourself: "Why, I would do everything in my power to lull the citizens of the United States into an apathetic and complacent attitude of euphoria and good spirits."

And this is precisely what the flaming leaves accomplish every fall. You will often see, as I have, grown men, solid respectable leaders of vast enterprises, dynamic participants in this free economy of ours, gazing at an oak or a sugar maple with looks of silly rapture on their faces.

If you ask them why, they will say that just looking at the beauty all around them makes them "feel good." We cannot afford for people to "feel good" in these desperate times, unless it is some accomplishment in Outer Space or the Middle East that inspires them. If the trees weren't showing off in this manner, there would be a lot more solid accomplishments this time of year.

But the heart of the matter is that this annual riot of color, this blaze of pigmentation in the countryside, is absolutely unregulated. Each state, each country, indeed each tree, goes its own way, without the aid of constructive planning from Washington.

Can we tolerate this sort of arboreal anarchism? To ask the question is to answer it.

No truly Great Society can depend on the whims of any species of vegetable, no matter how large.

My bill is not a radical one. It merely calls for the appointment of a committee to study ways and means for requiring that trees abandon their uncontrolled exhibitionism and, instead, make the contribution to our society of which, under proper federal supervision, I am sure they are capable. Thank you. (*Applause*)

Battle of the Dorm

Anyone who has observed a military operation, whether it was a major assault upon a fortified beach or a routine troop movement, has been amazed at the complexity of the logistics. How does everything get in the wrong place at the right time or vice versa? It takes staff work, I had always thought. Surely nothing could be that confused by accident.

I was, as it usually turns out, wrong. I was recently in the first wave to hit a girls' dormitory of a large university on check-in day. The innocence (or perhaps not) of eighteen-year-old scholars, female, and the dotings of their parents produced by chance a scene of chaos unrivaled by any ever achieved by the most careful calculations of the Joint Chiefs of Staff.

In what scenes of military hugger-mugger I have seen, my role has been unheroic, and at the Occupation of the Dorm I was also playing a menial part. I was a father.

I saw one fellow of my own grade, but not age, pull up. (My daughter always points out how much younger other girls' fathers look, and it's a straight line I wouldn't think of touching.)

Anyway, this fellow had a rental camper, towing a trailer. For two hours while I was unloading our car, he and I would pass each other.

Finally, I essayed a friendly approach, "Just about got her moved in, eh?"

"Well," he said, "I've got the trailer and half the camper emptied. But that just takes care of her hair. I haven't even touched the stuff for the child herself."

Seeing a grown man who may be a large vice-president of a bank somewhere, carrying a blow drier and a curling iron into a dormitory while he is being asked if he remembered to bring a few hundred other articles, which he doesn't know whether he has or not because he has no idea what they look like, is enough to arouse doubts about the structure of our society.

I would not want you to think that accoutrements for the hair were all that had to be moved in. I noticed dry-cleaning establishments fringing the campus. I don't know how they stay in business. Every girl had an outfit a day for the school year. Possibly that's an exaggeration, but the dress-per-girl ratio is a lot higher than it was when Grandma went off to Vassar with one valise.

The dormitory in the intellectual community of today is not the ivy-covered bungalow you may recall. It could easily be mistaken for a high-rise luxury motel. It is into a lobby of such elegance that a daddy struggles, with his fingers gradually being bent backward and broken by the weight of dress hangers.

Yes, dress hangers. That is the way you take the clothes to school, if you are stupid. You put them on hangers and hang them on a pole that stretches across the back seat. If you are stupid, but prudent, you part them a bit so you have some vague idea of the traffic behind you.

You know what's delightful? Sixty miles an hour and the pole falls down. It's a frightening sound in itself, but nothing in comparison with the screams of anguish that follow it.

You turn in at the next genuine pecan praline place and put the rod back up. It's good for 38.7 miles. Somewhere in New Mexico I found a spot that sells a substantial steel car pole that will stay up. Its location is my secret.

As I remember, my son said he was going to college and we said, "Good, when you get there write and tell us which one it is." And, I believe, he did too.

Girls are, thank goodness as we used to say, different. Uni-sex will never make it. They need all the sewing stuff and the—I don't know, it's all so mysterious to me I couldn't even make up a list. I saw fathers walking in carrying stuffed animals. A notary public with a panda. Boys don't take stuffed animals to college, unless they're worried that the draft will start again.

I talked to a father who, like me, had driven 2,000 miles or so to get his daughter settled in. We agreed that it was worth it and 97 percent of kids today are great. I got him up a few percentage points. He started off at 93.

Anyway, he said he and the missus would miss Francine Sue and the battery-powered blow drier on the long trip back. But he said there was one bright thing. He could light up a cigar without having Francine Sue blow the smoke back into his face!

❖❖❖❖

Have a Nice Day

The other day one to whom I am tied by bonds not of this earth let me have a check out of the checkbook. I don't know how it is at your house, but by us it used to be that everybody wrote checks and tried to remember to tell the coholder. Now, due to all that funny printing at the bottom of the check, a joint account has to work out of one book. Since most check-writing gets done at home, ever since—but never mind that—if I am going to perpetrate one I obtain it through proper channels.

This check was to satisfy an investment loss due to backing the wrong basketball team. I do not gamble.

As I was writing it out I noticed that in the upper left-hand corner was a small design bearing the dread legend: "Have a Nice Day."

I had not ordered checks with that motif. Those who don't even know me, as well as my bank, know that it is a sentiment foreign to my nature.

It was particularly galling to hand to a man who had bested me in a basketball investment a fiscal instrument wishing him a nice day.

Allowing for a few exceptions, and without getting cute about it, my experience has been that most transactions in which you give money to someone else are not happy or nice.

Furthermore, most of the checks that emanate from my account are addressed to soulless corporations, the main occupation of which is grinding the faces of the poor. Am I supposed to wish such an outfit a nice day?

Do I care, for example, whether the gas company has a nice day? I know that it is wishing all the while for a terrible day so that I will use more of its invaluable product.

So wouldn't the gas company think I was being sarcastic and maybe raise my bill just to show me who's boss, as if I didn't know?

As it happens I own a couple of shares in a farflung utility. It sells its stock only to widows and orphans, under the last of which categories I qualify.

Suppose I were to pay my bill to that utility while wishing it a nice day. Now remember that I labor for a free and independent press. Wouldn't critics of the latter call my credibility into question if I am throwing kisses at a corporate octopus which often has troubles which must be aired in print?

I am not by nature a grouchy man. "Sullen" is the word that is most commonly applied to the impression I make on people. But whatever may be the adjective, I am not the type to scatter wishes for a nice day incontinently across the landscape.

Especially where money is concerned.

If there are people for whom I wish a nice day I would prefer to be selective about it. If I stay at a terrible hotel and finally persuade them to turn loose of my luggage upon receipt of a personal check, the imprinted sentiment "Drop Dead" would suit my frame of mind better than "Have a Nice Day."

Another point. I might be asked by my wife to be a dear, as I often am, and write a fifteen-dollar check to Phoebe Jane Grundinger.

I don't know the lady. I don't know what the check is for. It may be for the Calm Chat club dues or for letting out or taking in seams or for winning an investment in basketball. I write the check to this strange, or anyway to me unknown, woman. And on the face of it appears the thing about having a nice day.

As I say, I don't know Phoebe Jane, but might she not misunderstand and call to suggest that we meet someplace dim for lunch until first thing you know, we are helpless in the grip of a powerful emotion which causes me to miss some of my favorite TV shows?

Of course, I realize that this is unlikely to happen. Just as I know that when, a while back, I was talking about checks to giant corporations they mainly go to computers, and who knows what a computer's idea of a nice day is?

All I am asking is that the bank not stick editorial opinions on my checks. Should it be determined to do so, several come to mind which express the way I feel while writing most checks much better than, "Have a Nice Day."

❖❖❖❖

Public Listening

Programs for the improvement of the species abound in courses in public speaking. But in none of the adult education brochures do we find "What to Do While Listening to a Speech" listed as part of the curriculum.

And yet even in this day when public speaking ranks, as an industry, somewhere between chemicals and steel, there still must be more listeners than speakers.

You may think that listening to the inspiring message brought to us by our speaker today is a simple matter. This is not the case. Because it is against the rules of after-dinner listening ever to look at the speaker while he is talking.

Next time you are at a banquet, glance around during the speech. You will find a great deal of ceiling-studying going on. On some occasions ceiling students comprise the bulk of the audience, and speakers report that it is an unnerving experience to look out over the hall and see nothing but chins.

Inexperienced speakers, facing a broad sea of intelligent Adam's apples, sometimes fall into the error of directing an apprehensive eyeball upward, for fear that the ceiling is collapsing. This can cause them to lose their train of thought and has driven more than one tyro permanently from the lectern.

Studying the ceiling is not, of course, the only profitable thing that can be done while waiting for the speaker to get from his firstly to his fifteenthly. There is cigar-looking. The postprandial popularity of the cigar is not due solely, or even most importantly, to its value as a smoke. Men smoke cigars after public luncheons so they can look at them.

The way to do it is to put the cigar in your mouth, light it, and then take it out and gaze at it with an expression indicating that you have no idea what it is or how it got there.

After the first amazed scrutiny, you may puff on the cigar a few more times (while looking at the ceiling), then take it out and examine it again to see if it looks any different.

Often some differences do appear. The ash may have become longer and the rest of the cigar, consequently, shorter. This phenomenon requires quite a bit of study. If your neighbor does not have a cigar, hold yours so he can help you look at it. He'll appreciate it.

Another worthwhile thing to do is to make marks on the tablecloth with a fork. Some veteran luncheon club members carry their own forks in case the waitress should remove the silverware before the speeches start.

Marks with forks can be made all in one direction or can be gone over again at right angles for a pleasing waffled design.

During speeches is a good time to catch up on your reading. If there is a bottle of meat sauce on the table, the label will provide enough reading matter (if read slowly and reflected upon) to last through the chairman's introductory remarks and the speaker's first three jokes.

Quite a bit of matchbook reading goes on also. Speech listeners are avid consumers of this type of literature. An acquaintance who hears more speeches than the average man claims that he now knows the matchbooks of all the city's leading hotels and restaurants by heart, right down to "Close Cover Before Striking."

With these few simple techniques, anyone can be a good Public Listener and avoid the embarrassment of being caught looking at the speaker, which is not only a breach of etiquette but causes the speaker to fear that there is something unfortunate about his clothing or that you are trying to remember what he looks like so you can punch him in the nose after the meeting.

❖❖❖❖❖

Mug Shot

I suppose you have known people who always seem to be looking at themselves in any reflecting surface that comes within eyeshot. If they are women, and if it is still permissible to indicate that there are differences betwen the sexes, it can be put down as a pleasingly feminine vanity.

But when a man is observed to be catching sidelong glances at himself in cigarette machine mirrors or in store windows, the judgment is not quite so kind. Either he is some sort of popinjay or he is Basically Insecure.

The latter explanation is preferable because it is more fashionable. When confronted by behavioral aberrations of whatever kind the simplest diagnosis is to observe that the subject is Basically Insecure.

Still I must admit I was surprised to see an old friend gazing steadfastly into his wristwatch, obviously trying to study his own face. I had never thought of him as either.

Naturally I pressed him for an explanation.

"You may think I am conceited or Basically Insecure," he said, smiling sheepishly, "and maybe it's a little of both. But I think the main thing is plain old curiosity."

"You are curious about your face?" I asked.

"I never thought I was," he said. "After all I have been shaving it more or less every day for more years than I care to comment on. It never really interested me one way or another. I mean you have to have something on the front of your head, and from what I could see it was just about like any other face. But now I don't know."

"What has brought about the change?" I asked.

"You won't understand," he said, "unless you have a daughter who is an art student. Which I am proud to say I have."

"All this," I asked, "has something to do with your newborn interest in your face?"

"Yes," he said. "The other night she revealed that she had to produce a portrait, a sketch from life. The cat wouldn't hold still and everybody else was busy. Would I sit for her?

"I must admit that I was somewhat pleased. I said that I believed I could accommodate her and immediately put a cigar in my mouth and raised two fingers in a Churchillian pose. I held it for five minutes until I discovered she had gone out for a cookie and a glass of milk and had not yet begun the masterpiece.

"When she began work I strove for a more restrained composition, chin on fist, eyes fixed on some distant dream. Not too bad.

"The trouble was that she accompanied her drawing with audible comments on the model. It turns out that my nose is not like other people's. Somehow the way it fits into the general facial composition makes it very difficult, if not impossible to draw.

"I told her that if it would help she could put both eyes on one side of the nose, but she said her teacher didn't like Picasso and besides if I moved my lips again she'd have to start all over again. Then she asked me if my ears had always been like that. Because I didn't want to violate her instructions not to talk I didn't point out to her that the location of the human ear means that every man knows more about what his neighbor's ears look like than he does about his own.

"One of her opinions was that my entire head seems to have been put together with parts that don't quite fit. Sometimes she just giggled and called her mother over to share whatever the humor of the situation may have been.

"All this, mind you, from a girl who has always said she loved me and even, when she was quite small of course, said I was handsome."

"How did the sketch turn out?" I asked.

"She wouldn't let me see it," he said. "And I really don't care. But I don't think I'll ever feel the same about my face again. That's why every time I get a chance I try to get a look at it to try to figure out what's wrong. But at least I've learned one thing."

"What's that?"

"Never let somebody who loves you draw your picture."

Oh, Porn...

The word in intellectual circles is that pornography is passe. The pendulum has swung and the big payoff in fiction from now on is going to be for books that are wholesome and uplifting.

Good news, some may say, but it comes as a shock to a friend of mine who has written several books that sold modestly if at all.

He came by grumpily the other night to say that the trend toward fiction which would not bring a blush to the maiden cheek is a rotten trick being played on him by fate.

"All the time," he said, "that I was writing little clean books that didn't sell, other people were writing big dirty books that did. I told myself that I could write that kind of thing if I wanted to debase my talent. My publisher kept urging me to go ahead, debase it, since it wasn't worth very much to either him or me the way it was.

"So I said, what the heck, which was the kind of language I used in those days. What the deuce, I said to myself, I will take a quick wallow in the gutter and it will go for a million copies in paperback and the movies will snap it up."

"That's rotten of you," I told him, "but understandable."

"It was not only rotten," he replied, "but dumb. I said to the d- - -l with integrity, I would write one big, filthy block-buster and retire on the proceeds.

"The trouble was that when I sat down to write I discovered I didn't even know the words. When I looked them up I didn't understand the definitions. Apparently I hadn't Lived enough, that's with a capital L.

"I left my wife, had a tourist agency arrange an itinerary of highly recommended cesspools, and drained a dreg or two. I became a pornographic phenom."

"And still couldn't write the book?" I inquired.

"Oh, no," he said. "I wrote it all right. But no publisher

will even read past the first page. Dirt is out, they informed me."

"Maybe you could clean it up," I suggested.

"I tried that," he said. "But after I cut out the rancid parts there was nothing left but my byline and the dedication."

"Tough luck," I said.

"I think I should be able to sue somebody," he said. "I invested a lot of time and money in learning how to write with what the critics only a few brief months ago were hailing as brutal frankness. The least they could have done was warn me that brutal frankness was a perishable commodity. I wonder if I could deduct the cesspool tour from my income tax?"

"Probably not," I said.

"I suppose you're right," he sighed. "But I'll tell you this, it's awfully discouraging for a man to compromise his principles and then discover that there is no money to be made out of it."

"You have my sympathy, or a little of it anyway," I said. "Why don't you try reissuing those old books of yours, the clean ones?"

"I suggested that," he said, "but the publishers said I would be accused of trying to cash in on the current fad for clean books. They said it would look greedy and unprincipled."

"Well, then," I said, "you'll just have to write a new, clean book."

"That's what I'm trying to do," he said, "but I'm going to have to get a new typewriter. The one I have now has developed a simply shocking vocabulary."

We all, I suppose, have our problems.

Safety First

I have a friend who is going around with one foot in a cast, and he blames it all on an article his wife read about safety in the home.

Among the hazards portrayed was the cluttered basement stairway. Statistics on the number of injuries caused by falling over roller skates, boxes, mop handles, flower pots, basketballs, and pop bottles allowed to accumulate on the steps were reinforced by a vivid drawing of a breadwinner hurtling violently in the direction of a fracture if nothing worse. My friend's wife was impressed, and the next Saturday morning she pointed out to him that their own basement steps were virtually invisible because of the junk.

"Do you want to become a statistic?" she inquired.

"Yes," he answered, for all the good it did him, "I want to be part of the 8.9 percent of all American adult males who will be lying on the couch watching the football game on the teevy."

So he spent most of the day putting the shotgun shells in the basement, the picture frames in the attic, the garden hose in the garage and so on, with the tricycle and the dog's dish and the moosehead and all the rest, each in a place more appropriate than the basement stairs.

"I must admit," he told me, "that those stairs, free of impedimenta, were lovely. I had never really seen them before. Most of that stuff had been dropped there when we moved in."

My friend said that not only was he charmed by the esthetics of his newly uncovered staircase but he felt a surge of pride, knowing that he was protecting his family from accidents.

"It gave me," he said, "a warm feeling, like a papa bear guarding a cave."

What it also gave him was a broken ankle when he fell down the steps.

He was thus rather rudely introduced to a principle that some graduate student of safety engineering might expand into a doctoral thesis—some things are so dangerous that they are safe.

Nobody in this man's family had ever fallen down those basement steps—nor had the gas man or the water meter reader. One look at it and you knew this was a flight of stairs that called for alertness, for a firm hand on the railing. Each move of a foot in that mass of household litter was planned as carefully as though for an ascent of the north face (if that's the tough one) of the Matterhorn.

The minute the obvious peril was removed, of course, overconfidence set in, and he dashed blithely down the stairs and right into his present predicament.

I know of a street intersection that has this same built-in safety factor. It frightens everybody into extra caution. Motorists know that, like the cluttered basement stairs, it is nothing to be approached lightly.

Thus the very factors which might cause accidents actually prevent them. Or at least that is the way the theory runs.

My friend said that he appreciated my explaining the principle to him but he doubted if it would do any good to pass it along to his wife.

"I don't think she would let me reclutter those steps," he said gloomily. "Besides that, she has bought me a new ladder and thrown away my old, safe one."

"Why was it so safe?" I asked.

"It had a busted rung," he replied, "and it scared me so that I never fell off it. This new one is so much safer it's dangerous. Next time I wash the windows I'll probably break my neck."

And he hobbled off.

❖❖❖❖❖

Aunt Fern Pottle Reports on Watergate

You all remember Aunt Fern Pottle, formerly the correspondent for the Isosceles Community to the Oblong, Oklahoma, *Oboe*, who retired several years ago to Washington, D.C., where she makes her home with her daughter, Mrs. Zoe (Bun) Tump, her son-in-law, Jim Tom Tump, and her two lovely grandchildren. Shuffling through our files we discovered the following missive which dates from 1974. It should be of considerable interest to Aunt Fern's many friends.

Old friends at home may wonder if Mrs. Fern Pottle, who now makes her home in the Capital of the Free World, has been indicted (hah! hah!). Actually she has been too busy with her needlepoint and running down the Pottle family tree at the Library of Congress to pay much attention.

Fredonia and Cal Sitzbark from over New Triangle way were recent visitors to these environs. Cal, who does important work for a group of milk producers, visited Capitol Hill, to which Mrs. Fern Pottle directed him by bus.

They brought welcome word of doings back home.

Mrs. Fern Pottle, a professional Penwoman for more than 40 years, does not understand the Press in Washington, where she now shares the luxurious and well-appointed home of Mr. and Mrs. Jim Tom and Zoe (Bun) Tump. The latter will be remembered as nee Pottle.

When she first took pen in hand, Mrs. Fern Pottle was told by Cameron Follansbee, founder and prop. of the Oblong *Oboe*, who had worked in Muskogee and elsewhere, never to limit her writings in the Isosceles Items column to the same circle of people. She, by all accounts, learned her lesson well and often printed the names of persons to whom she was not related.

The Press in Washington, on the other hand, seems to pay attention, day in and day out, to a small group of men who must have coffee together every morning, and maybe their wives belong to the same Sunbeam Sisterhood. The Old Editor would never have stood for it.

Many of the persons prominently mentioned in the papers here are in the political line of work. Very little such was featured in the Isosceles Items column under Mrs. Fern Pottle. By the time Sunday visitings, hospital reports, and club meetings were reported there was very little room for talk of those in the political line, many of whose folks asked that their names be kept out of the paper.

Rather surprising was the action of Richard Nixon, perhaps no relation to some people of that name whom old-timers may remember as running the cafe next to the Conoco station at one time, in blaming some sort of problems with his Dictaphone on his secretary. In the old days if Miss Daisy Funkbinder at Crenshaw's Sundries made a mistake on a bill why Mr. Al Crenshaw would smooth it over and not say a word to Miss Daisy for fear she would be confined to her home for three or four days.

Mr. and Mrs. Cal Sitzbark (I think she was a Noonan) were

told by Mrs. Fern Pottle when they were here that much of the trouble here is caused by nobody knowing anybody else's folks.

Back around the old home area if somebody had known your dad there wasn't any doubt about you, and if anybody did anything wrong it was kept quiet until he left town.

But in Our Nation's Capital nobody knows anything about anybody's family (even though it could be checked in the Library of Congress) and so there is a lot of trouble, which is all in the papers, which just stirs people up, whereas the performance of Sean Tump, adorable grandson of Mrs. Fern Pottle, as a soybean in his school pageant went unnoticed.

This way of regarding what is important to splash across the front page makes Mrs. Fern Pottle miss the old home place and dear hearts, although Jim Tom and Zoe (Bun) Tump have a new color television.

❖❖❖❖

Yet Another Report from Aunt Fern Pottle
Circa 1973

All Washington is buzzing over the enthusiastic reception given to Mrs. Fern Pottle's appliqued potholders at the charity bazaar of the Baptist Church where several Secretaries of the Interior have been known to worship. They were almost snatched from the hands of the volunteer ladies by many who said nothing their equal was available on F Street, which is to Washington what Muskogee Avenue is to Oblong.

Those who recall Mrs. Fern Pottle's potholders will appreciate that the most demand at the charity bazaar was for her tomato pattern with the daisy not far behind. Several of both patterns are in daily use in homes throughout Kigowah County, Oklahoma, where they will be remembered by many as having been featured at fairs and bazaars.

A souvenir plate purchased at the Peoples Drugstore by Jim Tom Tump at the request of his mother-in-law, Mrs. Fern Pottle, has been sent to Benicia Droog for her approaching nuptials with Drexel Angnangle.

It shows the likenesses of President Richard Milhous Nixon and his lovely wife together with their daughters, Julie and Patricia. It is to be hoped that this historic replica will find a niche in the honeymoon home that Benicia and Drexel will share with his parents, with whom the bridegroom will be associated in farm loans and appliances.

It is certainly a small world, as has often been remarked. On the same day as the Droog-Angnangle exchange of vows, the Nixons' daughter, Patricia (known to most as Tricia), will be married to Edward Cox.

(It may have already happened by the time you read this, the mails being what they are, not like when Oran Baxley had the rural route from Oblong to Isosceles and back across all the country south of the Big Gritty River, and always on time with a cheery word, and yet they are raising the price of stamps so that many old friends at home may go unremembered by Mrs. Fern Pottle on their birthdays, to all of whom God bless.)

Although Mrs. Fern Pottle has not been invited to any of the festivities, since she has only lived in this community a short while with her daughter Zoe (Bun) Tump and her son-in-law, Jim Tom Tump, there has been much about it in the local papers which come out once a day.

The Nixon girl and her intended are a handsome couple. She appears to be lighter complected than Benicia Droog. Eddie Cox, as many call him, looks quite a bit like Drexel Angnangle around the eyes, as nearly as can be told because the wedding pictures here were not taken by Mr. Klamm of Oblong who took Zoe (Bun) Pottle's pictures when she was wed to Jim Tom Tump and would not quit snapping away

179

until everyone was satisfied. In larger communities, I suppose, they cannot take the time to get things exactly right. Everything is Rush! Rush! Rush!

Although neither the Nixon nor Cox families are well-acquainted in the Isosceles area, it will be remembered that Judge Cranston Beal was a delegate to the convention that nominated the bride's father to High Office, so it is imagined that there will be considerable interest.

The wedding will be held at home, which is often done in Oklahoma, although seldom in the backyard, which is the plan if it doesn't rain.

Mrs. Fern Pottle will not go to the wedding, which is too bad, judging from the description of the wedding cake. Her own heirloom recipe will be used when Drexel marries Benicia, and if Mrs. Fern Pottle had her choice between the two—but she doesn't.

She wishes both young couples all the happiness she found with the late Mr. Pottle, whom many dear hearts at home will recall.

❖❖❖❖

The Nonaggression Look

In a brief ramble through the women's news I was pleased to discover that a top Paris fashion designer is producing "unaggressive" clothes. This is what this old world needs in these troubled times. Too many clothes are loud and pushy.

It's just as true of men's clothes as of women's, maybe even more so.

You won't believe this, but at one time I had a green tweed suit. It was in a violent plaid. You may think that the adjective only applies to a violent clash of colors. But this suit was violent in the physical sense of the word.

When I opened the closet door it would grab me around the throat.

"You wear me today, boy," it gritted in my ear, "or you're in a heap of trouble."

I hated that suit but I wore it an awful lot, much as I preferred the blue serge which was the other half of my wardrobe. The blue serge was a great suit but it wasn't aggressive. As far as it was concerned it could hang in the closet week after week, counting the coat hangers.

It was such an unaggressive serge suit it never even got shiny. And what's more it didn't care.

Fighting off the clutches of that green tweed for all those years (it was not only aggressive but wore like iron) turned me against aggressive clothes altogether.

In a day when everything is bold, from beer to the front grille of the car, there certainly is a place for something that is unaggressive in our society.

Clothing would seem a reasonable place to start. Why should we be bullied by our haberdashery?

Aggressive clothing, I suspect, has a bad effect on the wearer. I know that when I was wearing that green tweed I was not nearly as nice a person as when I had on the blue serge.

I smoked cigars, even lighting them in elevators, talked loudly, slapped people on the back, and thought of buying an imitation diamond pinkie ring. In the blue serge, on the other hand, I was reserved, quiet, a bit shy, puffing on a sedate brier pipe.

People who saw me in the two different suits often wouldn't believe I was the same person.

"It is I," I would reassure them. "It is just that I am wearing my unaggressive suit today."

"Praise be," they were likely to respond.

If clothing can be sold on the basis that it is unaggressive, maybe the same appeal would work on other products.

181

Mouthwash, for example, is touted as being bold, which is the same as aggressive. It might be great for the breath, but the picture I get is of somebody who can hardly wait to get out of the house in the morning so he can breathe on people.

Why can't we have a retiring mouthwash, one that goes quietly about his job?

And, of course, automobiles look aggressive. They snarl. That, presumably, is why people buy them.

Maybe we could test that theory by advertising:

"Drive the polite car. The unaggressive one which says to others, 'After you.'"

Perhaps that's asking too much. Still, if we can start out with unaggressive clothes, who knows where it might lead?

❖❖❖❖

Leafing Through America

This is the time of year when it is customary for Americans to go out and make inspections of the autumnal glory which is marching like an army with banners across the hills. In other words, look at the leaves.

Many people travel hundreds of miles to spots that are notorious for the brilliance of their fall foliage. The reason for going all that distance is so they can complain that the trees aren't half as pretty as the ones in their own backyard.

There seems to be a certain satisfaction in reaching this conclusion. Natives are often surprised by tourists yelling at them out of the car: "You got rotten leaves."

These people don't necessarily mean to be rude or unappreciative. It is just one of the things that tradition has decreed should be said on the occasion of looking at trees in the fall.

There are other choices, of course. One of them is:

"If an artist were to paint those colors you wouldn't believe it."

Everybody has at least one aunt who always has said that about not believing autumn's colors if an artist were to paint them. They often say the same thing about sunsets.

Uncle Fred got so tired of hearing his wife, Oleander June, make that remark that he took her to an art gallery where there was a beautiful painting of an autumn landscape. Aunt Oleander June said she didn't believe it.

But anyway that's an O.K. thing to say about the seasonal scenery.

So many people who are new at tree-viewing find it hard to keep the conversation going. One good idea is to say, "Oh, look at that scarlet tree up there." Say it to the driver just as he is rounding a curve. Wives will often scream at husbands to look at that scarlet tree.

"Yeah, I saw it," the husband may reply if he succeeds in not running off the road.

"No you didn't. It was scarlet. Right at the top of the hill."

"I saw it."

"You didn't see it. You just say you saw it because you're jealous. Anyway, if you did see it, I saw a better one that I didn't tell you about."

As you can imagine this sort of talk about the trees can brighten an afternoon's drive through the environment. It can make an hour's spin seem as though it had been going on for days.

Another approach to the situation is to compare this year's coloring with last year's.

"Well, the trees are nice," you may say, "but nothing like as pretty as they were last October when we drove down to see Maude and Cicil."

"Yeah, but they're better than they were the year we went to the football game that time whenever it was."

If this exchange isn't sparkling enough for you, just wait

183

awhile. Somebody is sure to get into his version of the scientific reasons why the leaves are better some years than others. The word "photosynthesis" will add class to the conversation.

Then, too, leaves are like fishing. There is always the opportunity to speculate that they would have been better (or worse) last weekend than this or that they will be better (or worse) a week from now.

Interesting discussions can be started as to whether a particular tree is, in fact, russet, scarlet, crimson, or any hue in that vicinity.

These various elements can be combined into a sort of running commentary which makes a trip to see the leaves a fascinating experience. It also explains why so many people get left behind at filling stations.

❖❖❖❖

One-Topic Towns

I recently spent a pleasant day in Lincoln, Nebraska, and came away reflecting on how nice it is to visit a one-topic town.

In many communities the outsider finds himself thrust among strangers, warm and hospitable though they may be, with whom he has difficulty establishing rapport because there is some uncertainty as to just where their interests lie.

Lincoln provides the ultimate in amenities for the visitor. There is no hesitation as to what to talk about, none of that tiresome and even embarrassing floundering about for ways to start a conversation.

What you talk about is football. Nor do you have to know anything about football to participate. Everything, as the British say, is laid on. Opinions are provided for you.

You are, of course, not expected to talk about football in general. The conversation is very specifically about the team of the University of Nebraska and why it is No. 1 in the nation.

Something similar, I am told, is true in Norman, Oklahoma. I have not been there recently and I hesitate to report anything of which I do not have firsthand knowledge, but informants I believe reliable assure me that Norman, like Lincoln, is a one-topic town. The same topic, of course, only with an obvious difference.

(Check your ticket stubs closely. When discussing football it is important to know whether you are in Oklahoma or Nebraska.)

I am afraid that the one-topic town is fading from the American scene. As we diversify and homogenize and polarize and interreact and do all those other sociologically complex things, it is increasingly difficult to arrive in a community and figure out what subject would be good to bring up for lunch table discussion.

At one time, for example, a man could breeze into Danbury, Connecticut, and talk about hats or drop by Hartford and go into what's new in extended coverage. I doubt if it is that simple any more.

Visit Memphis today and you will find those who not only don't know the price of cotton but don't want to hear about it. Smog, once a sure topic in Pittsburgh, has been pre-empted by the rest of the country.

Hollywood used to be a snap. You merely talked about movies, what starlet was going with which producer, and who was jetting in from the Main Stem to ink a pact.

Now all the movies are made in Yugoslavia or someplace very like it, and I couldn't even guess what they talk about in Hollywood, if there still is such a place.

Of course there are still some one-topic cities. In New York there is no problem. You are expected to talk about how

185

terrible New York is. Keep plucking at that one string and you can get along very nicely.

In San Francisco similarly, or rather conversely, you talk about how wonderful San Francisco is.

I'm not sure about Detroit. Do they talk solely about automobiles there? Or do they talk more about Ralph Nader? It could be that they are sick of both subjects.

Washington, D.C., is, of course, the pre-eminent one-topic town. The subject is politics at breakfast, lunch, and dinner, and between meals, as well. I see no danger that the recent infusion of culture into our Nation's Capital will cloud the crystal stream of political talk.

I must admit that this new excitement about the Washington Redskins is disturbing. Is one now expected to talk football when he goes to Washington? I don't think so. My hunch is that conversation about the Redskins is restricted to counsenting indigenous personnel. Outsiders are not expected to get involved. Unless the foundations of the way of life we have known are to be irreparably shattered there is no conversational confusion in Washington for the man who sticks to politics.

One-topic towns are wonderfully relaxing places to visit and the decline in their numbers cannot but grieve those who have enjoyed them in the past. This is why I recommend a visit to Lincoln (or possibly Norman). But hurry before the football season ends and they become just like any other multitopical city.

❖❖❖❖

God Didn't Make This Tree!

At the risk of causing the late Joyce Kilmer to revolve, I must admit that there is a tree I hate. Hatred of any kind is an ugly thing. And to hate, or even dislike, a tree is worse. Trees—like mother, flag, and Eleanor Roosevelt—are

186

customarily spoken of only with affection and esteem. Especially in the autumn, when arborolatry is rampant.

This is the time of year when entire families drive hundreds of miles, consuming untold gasoline and peanut butter sandwiches, just to look at trees.

I like trees. Let's get the record straight on that. Never before have I knocked a tree. They have sent their roots through my soil pipe, clogged my gutters with their leaves, and kept my bluegrass from growing.

But I have never said a word. I have looked for their good qualities, of which trees have many. Trees give shade against the summer heat, they provide choir lofts for our feathered friends, they—but why go on? If we were to list all the nice things about trees, there would be no end to it.

I like trees. But not this tree.

This tree, which is in my backyard, is a slob. More than that it is a malevolent slob.

This tree hates *me*. So what am I supposed to do—love it in return? That would, of course, be the Christian thing, but it lies beyond the capabilities of my sinful nature.

It hates me, this tree does, and I hate it back.

Don't ask me what kind of tree it is. I don't know its name; I don't want to know.

When I encounter a man who smokes a loud cigar on a tightly closed bus, I don't care what his name is. I don't want to know him. I don't want to know the name of the referee who calls back what would have been my team's winning touchdown, or the man who does the stomach acid commercials on television, or the lady who goes shooby-shooby on a rock-'n'-roll record, or the people who stick those little subscription cards in magazines, or the inventor of bubble gum.

Their names are unnecessary to me, and I feel the same way about this tree.

It is a big tree. A big, mean tree.

Here is what it does.

Every year, when other trees are turning scarlet or gold or purple or what not, this tree does nothing. It just squats there with its big, ugly branches loaded down with the same dull-colored leaves.

Other trees permit their leaves to float gently, caressingly to earth. They fall like a benediction upon the shoulders of the man who is raking the yard in the crisp and winelike October air. Gathered into piles, these leaves attract the adventurous child to play with joyful cries and the little dog to romp and laugh its woffy laughter.

This tree does not let go of its leaves. It hoards them, clings to them, and watches with evil pleasure as the yard is raked, the gutters cleaned, the leaves barreled or burned.

Then, when all the work is done, when the yard is immaculate, the last leaf gone, this miserable slob of a tree lets go its leaves. Not gently, not gradually or poetically.

All at once—thunk!

In one night they all come down and the yard is two feet deep in this thing's leaves.

These leaves are indescribable, at least by me. They seem to be made out of some sort of synthetic leather. Whatever they are, they are fireproof.

Put them in a burner and they will not burn. They will smolder and exude an aroma unsmelled since Uncle Ed used to put his galoshes on the andiron.

At other times of the year this tree does other unpleasant things, such as dropping squishy purple fruit on people or littering an entire block with seed pods.

People have tried to tell me that this is a mulberry tree, but I refuse to listen to them. I wouldn't want to say that it is a mulberry tree and give mulberry trees a bad name. I believe that every tree, like every person, should be judged on its own, regardless of race, creed, or color. It is this particular tree I am talking about. If it is a mulberry tree, there is no reason to publicize the fact, because other mulberry trees are undoubtedly as disgusted by its behavior as I am.

Mulberry trees cannot be all bad; silkworms love them. Not even a silkworm could love this tree.

Joyce Kilmer never saw a poem as lovely as a tree, and I have never seen (except once or twice) a poem as ugly as this tree. It is a terrible tree.

❖❖❖❖

The Dishwasher Conspiracy

You awaken in the night and hear the sounds and you tell yourself that it's the old house settling, or maybe the wind in the trees. But is's not, and the chances are that it isn't ghosts either.

What it is is the appliances in the place talking to each other.

For years it was thought that machines had no feelings and were incapable of independent thought. Of course, the same thing used to be believed about plants. Now everybody but a few superstitious people realizes that a dishwasher is as mentally alert as the brightest African violet you may meet.

Not only do machines think but they scheme and conspire. This shows that they have reached a rather advanced stage in the intellectual process. It wasn't until several centuries after man learned how to think that it occurred to him to get together with his friends to plot dirty deeds against his unfriends. Which is how civilization, as we know it today, was born.

Now that any misconceptions about the ability of allegedly inanimate objects to think has been cleared up, we can get on with an examination of these colloquies that go on every night when the house's human occupants are assumed to be asleep.

The most obvious result of their scheming is that all the appliances go on strike at once. If the picture tube on the TV fades and dies you might as well figure on a new clothes drier, extensive repairs to the dishwasher, and stand by for the imminent collapse of the water heater.

The householder who thinks these events are unrelated coincidences is living in a fool's paradise. (Although, come to think of it, that can't be right because in a fool's paradise everything would work fine.)

No, my friends, this is an organized conspiracy. These devices which have infiltrated our homes under the guise of being our obedient and unthinking servants act in unison to do us in.

I wish to make it clear that I am not mounting some Ralph Nader type assault on the quality of our major appliances. (Get that word "major" with its subtle sneer of superiority.) Household machinery is no better and no worse than anybody else.

And that is the point that the consumer advocates miss. They blindly assume that machines go wrong because they were doomed from the first by shoddy manufacturing methods. This view may be regarded as the preordination wing of the philosophy of appliances. As a matter of cold, and sometimes hot, fact, the behavior of machines is much more a matter of free will.

Things break down because they decide to break down. Otherwise how could they all collapse simultaneously?

Furthermore they make their move when we are at our most vulnerable, when the bank account is at low tide, when we have house guests or are trying to get away on a vacation. And they always make their move on a weekend when help, if available at all, comes at double the customary fee.

Who knows most about us? Our appliances. The garbage disposal can tell when we are scrimping on food. If it wants a second opinion it can consult with the refrigerator. The

190

washing machine is aware that our clothes are frayed and patched.

So the word is passed from machine to machine in those midnight whispers and rustlings: "These kids are hurting bad; let's give it to them good."

And "Blonk" goes everything, including what remains of your cash on hand. There is no way to fight it, of course; we need the appliances more than they need us.

And, boy, do they know it.

❖❖❖❖

Halloween Modern-Style

It may be that we are going to have to rethink the whole matter of Halloween. The old spooks and hobgoblins just aren't scary any more. There is so much to alarm the citizen and his family in the daily course of events that it is really too much to expect anybody to get unduly exercised about a black cat. The only frightening thing about a pumpkin is the price it brings at the store.

Much of the spookiness of the old Halloween symbols has been dispersed by television, where ghosts are the result of faulty tuning and witches turn out to be nice, chatty ladies who appear on the late-night talk shows.

Possibly the only way to frighten the modern child would be to put on a TV repairman's uniform and say that you've come to take the set away.

Scaring grown-ups is easier, but again requires a little more imagination than the old skeleton or Dracula routine.

One possibility that suggests itself is to knock on a neighbor's door and say, "Glad I caught you in, Sam. This envelope from the IRS was delivered to my house by mistake. It looks important."

A man who has stood up to a barrage of Frankenstein monsters and Martians is going to quail.

Or you could show up at a man's front door, holding an automobile fender in your arms, and inquire, "I beg your pardon, but is this yours?" The warmest blood will experience at least a momentary chill.

You don't have to dress up in weird and horrid costumes to frighten your neighbors. Instead, put on your formal clothes, go from door-to-door, and cry cheerfully, "Hi. This is the night of your party, isn't it?"

This is a guaranteed shocker, especially if the neighbor is in his pajamas and robe.

Not quite as effective, perhaps because it is more complicated, is to show up carrying a surveyor's transit:

"Hope you don't mind, sir. Just a preliminary survey. Interstate's going to come right through your living room you know."

It is bound to shake up the victim, even if he eventually figures out not much surveying is done at night.

Wives who wish to throw a little Halloween fear into their husbands can ring their own doorbell, look out and exclaim, "Why, Henry, it's my sister's boy, Kevin Bob, with the cute beard and the bare feet and carrying a great big suitcase along with his guitar, come to pay us a visit."

That's going to send the old gentleman up to tuck his head under the covers like no papier mache ghoul ever did.

Another idea is to rouse a friend and say, "Too bad you missed the meeting tonight, Fred. You were named chairman of the fund-raising committee."

Then ask him to turn around so you can see the hair standing up on the back of his neck. It's quite a sight.

All in all, I think these are comparatively mild, but if making the blood run cold is what you're after, they are going to work a lot better than a tired old jack-o'-lantern.

NOVEMBER

A Note to Future Generations

Dear Professor: I am addressing you as professor because surely whatever else happens to civilization, the Ph.D. will survive. In fact, it may be that the Ph.D.s will take over the world, instead of the roaches that, heretofore, have attracted most of the smart money.

Be that as it may, and even if you are only a graduate student working toward your doctorate, I respect you as I do all archaeologists. I should think that there would be nothing more fascinating than rummaging around in the ruck and rubble of the remains of a vanished race and trying to reconstruct what those old people were like and what in the world they thought they were doing anyway.

For example, you come up with a ring that you say is what the court ladies of the Fan Tan dynasty wore in their noses, and your article is the smash hit of the June issue of the *Archaeological News.* Then some wise guy at Harvard says you are a fraud or at best a hoax perpetrator and that this is either a pawn used in a game by children during the pre-Columbian era or part of the door-latch mechanism of a 1926 Essex. As I say, fascinating.

What I want to get across, Professor, is that I feel a real empathy for archaeologists, so anything that I can do to lighten the load is the least I can give in return for all the pleasure I have gotten out of reading various archaeological flashes and bulletins through the years.

Which is why I have written this letter and put it in this tin box where I keep all the important stuff like, well let's see, the guarantee for an electric mixer that wore out ten years ago, a recipe pamphlet from a company that makes rum which I hate, an insurance policy, the receipt for the license on a long-departed dog, and so on. It's hard to say how long this tin box will survive the ultimate end of things, but I'd say it has about the best chance of anything in the house.

One word about that, though. If, by one of those freaks of history, this house should be preserved as perfectly as, say, Pompeii, you may not ever find this letter. There are an awful lot of boxes in this house. Most of them are empty.

I'm not expecting everything to be wiped out, of course—not for a few centuries. But in case something should happen pretty soon, I want to explain about the boxes. In case you find this note. Which, considering all the boxes, you may not.

I am assuming that you are a dedicated archaeologist. A man just about has to be, doesn't he? I mean, to be in the business at all. Because I'm pretty sure that one thing won't have changed in the however many centuries it will have been between the time I write this and the time you read it. You scholars and teachers are still underpaid. Am I right?

The thing you are going to wonder about is why the average home in the United States of America (which is where what you are standing on used to be) had all these empty boxes. Many an average United States of America husband wonders the same thing.

If, as I say, you are dedicated (which, on account of the low pay, you are bound to be), you are going to start opening all these boxes. And you are going to find most of them empty.

194

Especially if you are digging down from the top. This means you will hit the attic first. And that's all solid empty boxes. Worse than that, there are empty boxes within empty boxes within, etc.

Eventually, dedicated or no, you are going to get tired of opening boxes and finding nothing inside except nothing—or maybe another empty box. So you may give up and not ever open this box and miss the note, which would be an archaeological pity.

Because you will write a monograph about the significance of empty-box worship in our civilization and you have several chances of being wrong. You may think that these empty boxes represent our ancestors, or are a form of currency.

But the plain fact is that the average house has all these empty boxes because the average wife thinks that someday she will need them to put things in. She never does, and this, as you can see, is why the boxes pile up.

Well, what I started out to warn you about was that a big fad right now is reconstructing colonial villages and old country stores and forts and castles and riverboats and who knows what all, and I can see how they are going to mess you up if you get these tourist attractions confused with the real thing.

I mean, what are you going to make of a log blockhouse with a TV aerial on the roof, or a Wild West frontier town with a parking lot?

But I'll have to write you another note about that. I got off, as you see, on this empty-box thing, and already this letter is pretty long, considering that the language will probably be obsolete when you find this (if you do) and it's going to be one heck of a job deciphering it. I hope you think it was worth it.

❖❖❖❖

"And There's a 5 Percent Chance That It Won't Snow...."

A few years ago when the weather bureau started issuing something it called the Discomfort Index, which combined heat and humidity in a formula to give us the official word as to how we were enjoying the summer, there were civic protests. Many communities preferred to think of it as a Comfort Index, as having a more positive ring to it.

Why can't we have more of this attitude at other times of the year? We get these forecasts that are designed to make the approaching weather sound terrible. This country, let us remind ourselves, was not built by people who thought tomorrow was going to be punk. It was built by people who had the optimistic faith that tomorrow would, somehow, be better.

It didn't turn out that way too often, but the thing to remember is the optimism, the rejection of negative thinking.

What we have now is the weather bureau telling us, in effect, "Folks, there is a terrible, fierce blizzard on the way and you're going to hate it."

How much pleasanter it would be if we would rephrase it something like this:

"Guess what, folks! When you wake up in the morning and look out the window you will be greeted by a veritable fairyland of white. The lovely virginal snow, which comes highly recommended to us by leading poets, will transform streets and highways from their customary dullness into winter wonderlands. And best of all, this beauty will accumulate to a depth of eight generous inches."

This is the kind of forecast that would make us look forward eagerly to the next morning and we would spring from our beds to see if it had truly happened, instead of dragging ourselves out to groan "Oh, no" at the sight of the way the family sedan at the curb is just a bump in the snowscape.

The police and highway patrol tell us to stay home when there is ice and snow on the roads, which may be a good idea, but they emphasize the scary element by pointing out that we may slide into a ditch or some other unpleasantness.

It would be better, psychologically speaking, if we were advised along these lines:

"Here's a great idea, friends! Why not telephone the shop that you won't be in today and stay home and have one of those simply great family days, with corn-popping and parcheesi or maybe taking from the shelf some well-loved old book and reading aloud to the kiddies? Just think how lucky we are to be living in a climate where once in a while we get an opportunity for a rousing experience such as this.

"Or if you feel you simply have to get out on the roads, there are going to be some really outstanding chances to meet some fine new friends. The people who man the nation's tow trucks, for example, are among the greatest folks you'll ever want to meet. When they eventually get to you, chances are you'll find that they are warmhearted and with a smile for one and all.

"Driving today has practically a surefire guarantee that you will meet some of these splendid folks, to say nothing of snowplow crews and maybe a helicopter pilot if you have to be plucked from a drift.

"Another dividend from the condition of the roads is that the odds are excellent that you will be hopelessly marooned about a mile from the nearest habitation. If you make it to the farmhouse, you are likely to meet the wonderful family that lives there and you will be invited in for a bowl of hot soup, if their electricity happens to be working."

Communities with this kind of weather need to learn to treat it as an asset instead of taking it with so much grimness.

People can learn to enjoy almost anything, once they're persuaded that the official line is that it's supposed to be fun.

❖❖❖❖

Not to Mention Free Checking

I noticed that this old pal was looking rather haggard and unslept, and when I asked him about it he said it was because of the lumps in his mattress caused by the money he keeps there.

"Well," I said, "why don't you take your money to the bank? Are you old-fashionedly suspicious?"

"No," he replied. "I am shy."

"Shy?"

"Shy," he said. "And insecure. I don't know whether I could live up to the demands of the modern banking relationship."

I asked him what he meant and he spoke along these lines:

"They're so friendly. I read and see and hear the ads, and all the banks are sitting there waiting to take me by the hand, put an arm around my shoulder, and really understand my problems. I ask myself why they would do this. They must want me to love them in return. I love banks in the sense that I love filling stations or post offices or hardware stores. I mean I have nothing against them. Live and let live is my motto and we are all put here to get along with one another according to the inscrutable plan.

"But life today is a continuous emotional drain. A man works hard all day, he loves his wife and his children and his cousins as far as the second remove. He is faced every day with a new nation or oppressed section of an old one that he must sympathize with.

"So he gets in the habit of crossing the street when he walks by a bank. I mean I know that my money would be safer there than in the mattress, but I just don't want to get emotionally involved.

"They keep telling me that they want to give me a free ball-point pen, or a silver service, or if not a bicycle for my child, at least a balloon. It's embarrassing. You sort of feel that if you go into a bank they'll be warmhearted and friendly, but won't they really be wondering whether you are there out of reciprocal warmth and friendship or because you want a ballpoint pen?

"I have these nightmares, which is why I cross the street away from the bank, that they are sending vice-presidents out to drag me in off the sidewalk and force money on me.

"Maybe this is silly of me. But I feel that friendship is a two-way street, know what I mean? I just wouldn't be comfortable, taking all these things from the bank and not giving anything."

"You could give the president a ballpoint pen," I said. "Or a balloon."

"I tried that," he said. "It was the last time I opened a savings account and I got a cigar and an orchid to take home to my wife. Well, the next day I took a jar of jelly by the bank for the president, and his secretary said she would give it to him. I thought she was kind of chilly and asked her if she wasn't interested, like their advertising said, in my personal problem. 'You really have one, don't you?' was her answer.

"So I took my money out of that bank, and it's all in the mattress."

"You thought they were not properly appreciative of the jelly?" I asked.

"No," he went on, "I knew that these were kindly folks. Remember when bankers were bankers? Not any more. Now they are folks. And I got to thinking that when that girl gave the president the jelly he would have his wife call up my wife and invite us over for dinner, and then we'd have to have them back, and he could deduct it because I was a customer, but I couldn't afford to have this banker and his wife over for dinner out of my own pocket every other week or so.

"And I know enough about the new image of banking that he would be looking at me reproachfully every time we met and wanting to know why I hadn't dropped by in the last few days to pick up some more money. It's kind of uncomfortable sleeping on that cash, I'll admit. But it beats lying awake thinking about some friendly, folksy, kindly banker I had accepted a ballpoint pen from and then not even given him the courtesy of letting him lend me any money.

"I used to get along just wonderful with bankers when they were flinty-hearted and cold-eyed and throwing orphans out in the snow. But now I don't dare go near them. They are too nice."

We parted company, he back to stuff some more money in his mattress and I to my bank to pick up some free matches and weigh myself on the scale in the lobby.

The Joys of 30° Below Zero

As winter closes its grip on much of this great land of ours, I think it is time to emit some sort of a sunbeam. The purpose is to convince those who are locked in by snow, ice, and small children in damp garments that they are better off than they would be lolling on a tropic shore.

It is a challenge.

In order to face it properly I winged my way to paradise and back, taking notes for approximately five seconds of the time.

First of all, I think all those in frozen climes should realize that part of their precious heritage is freedom from the pineapple. To fend off a starchy note from Mr. Dole (not the Kansas senator, but the one in Hawaii) I must say that I enjoy his delicious fruit. But in the tropics it becomes terribly ubiquitous.

(Incidentally if the pineapple folk want to get mad at somebody, let them go sue Webster, who describes the product as "a sorosis consisting of the succulent fleshy inflorescence and that ripens into a solid mass invested with the tough persistent floral bracts.") Knowing Sam Webster as I do, I assume that this is an accurate outline of the plight of the pineapple, but it is not the kind of copy that is going to motivate you to rush down to the supermarket and buy a bunch. ("Ah, my dove, would you care for a sorosis of fleshy inflorescence?")

But to get back to the matter of ubiquity, it is what makes any vegetable or fruit a little too much, no matter how appealing it may be on a take-it-or-leave-it basis. The tomato has succumbed to ubiquity in our society, which is only gradually recovering from it. There was a period in our history (you can look it up) where you couldn't order anything in a restaurant without a tomato being mixed up in it somehow.

The pineapple is much the same in Hawaii. I had (still have) a brother who was addicted in his youth to pineapple ice cream sodas. But even he would not have put pineapples in otherwise semi-potable alcoholic beverages, which is what they do in the islands. They also put pineapples on anything edible. Except mashed potatoes. They put orchids on mashed potatoes. I'll tell you, Eden palls after you have eaten a lifetime supply of orchids in three days.

So what we have here in Frigid City is liberation from pineapples and orchids.

Let's consider another facet. Step out of your front door into a fairy wonderland, with a blanket of white over all the world, and you may slip on the steps and discommode an ankle. But the chances that you will cut your foot on a sharp piece of coral are very slim. Almost nil.

Certainly you can put up with a considerable amount of cold weather if it means that you and your dear ones will be safe from coral cuts or octopus soup. (I tossed octopus soup in there sort of unannounced because I don't want to think about it.)

Mothers, look at it this way: The carpet is a mess with the slush being tracked in, but at least the kids are not bringing in sand as they would in gentler latitudes. Slush melts and may even be good for the rug, but sand has nothing to recommend it.

If someone would care to underwrite the project I would be glad to head for the equator to report in greater depth upon the horrors that lucky folk in the North are being spared right this minute. But at least I have given you a few blessings to be counting.

❖❖❖❖

Eternally Speaking

A gentleman asks me to contribute to a compendium he is assembling from various people asking them (loved ones aside) what person they would like to talk to in that life which may be assumed to exist after death.

Now this is not a new idea. It dates back to about the time when somebody thought it was cute to ask people what book or books they would take with them if cast ashore upon a desert island. (Smart alecks who said they'd take along a volume on how to build a raft were not allowed to play any more, which was O.K. with them.)

I want to help this gentleman with his project, but there are certain problems. I do not know how things are going to be Over There where the woodbine twineth. (I feel it is best not to use the phrases Up There or Down There, which would just complicate things.)

But let us assume, in our theologically naïve way, that things over there are pretty much like they are here. In certain respects much better, of course. But, still, there must be a certain amount of organization. You are going to have to check in, and there will be forms to fill out.

Anyway there will be a blank, "To whom do you wish to talk?" (*Whom* will flourish in the Hereafter if nowhere else.)

Well, you decide to give it your best shot and you put down "Samuel Johnson," generally regarded as the best conversationalist, in English anyway, who ever lived. Imagine the ease with which the Doctor could have obliterated Johnny Carson on a talk show.

Well, the angel, or whatever, would look over your papers and frown.

"About this conversation with Samuel Johnson," he or she would say. "I'm afraid that would be a bit awkward. He has been a very hot property for nearly two hundred years now.

"I might be able to work you in sometime during the twenty-first century, as you people figure it, but then about all you'll get is that one about a woman standing on her hind legs being like a dog preaching. The poor dear ran out of new lines about 1902 and is even getting his old ones wrong."

So you suggest Mark Twain or Walter Raleigh or Voltaire or Plato or Julius Caesar or Montaigne or W. C. Fields. But it's the same with all the really big talkers of history. They're booked solid. On a different plane, it would be like calling on H. R. (Bob) Haldeman, for a chat and he says that will be $25,000 money up front.

I don't mean that there would be anything commercial on that Farther Shore, but the talkers that everybody wants to talk to aren't going to have the time, even though they'll have all eternity, to talk to everybody.

I just can't see how you could tap a fellow spirit on the shoulder and say, "I know you. You're Newton and I'd like to talk about that apple business." You're liable to get back, "Some other time, Mac, I got the whole physics faculty of the University of Gothenburg been waiting here for centuries. Take a number."

I have spent enough time in this world waiting to see important or self-important people. So, when I get around to answering the book gentleman, I don't think I'll drop any of the large names on him.

I assume that Over There language obstacles will not occur and I will have no difficulty talking to the people I want to see. Considering the press of people around the more prestigious talkers, I think there should be no difficulty in approaching the people I want.

I'd like to have a conversation with one of the nameless bunch who built the pyramids or the ancient mounds of America. I'd like to know how they did it. If I could corner one of the blokes who put up Stonehenge I'd want to ask what he had in mind. The same with one of the ordinary hewers and carriers that got those big faces on Easter Island.

What could be better than an hour or so with one of Columbus's crew, finding out what kind of trip it was and whether they really thought the old man was crazy. Let me talk to an enlisted man at Hastings or Waterloo or Ypres to find out what he thought of how things went.

I could give up conversation with the great poets and authors in favor of sitting around with the printers who had to see the stuff and get their thinking.

On the other bank of that River in other words, I think I'll be the way I've been on this one, perfectly content without bothering the Big Folks.

❖❖❖❖

Character Mold

An ill-advised young man asked me the other day what agencies had contributed the most to molding my character. It was complimentary, unless he was being sarcastic, as it indicated that I had a character, no matter how mouldy.

I am afraid I let him down, being unable to do much more than mumble a few generalities about home, school, and church which, I suppose, played their part. But I don't think I was precise enough to be of any great help to him, which probably didn't matter much, since it was a classroom assignment.

Since then I have been giving it some thought.

First off, I would say that miniature golf was one of the great teachers of my generation. What did I learn from it? Well, we are not talking about what I learned, just about whether it made a contribution to the Ultimate Me.

Miniature golf taught me to shorten my swing in the Game of Life. Other people go for the 300-yard drive, the booming wood off the tee. I am content with thinking no long thoughts, only short ones, aiming for the nearest objective and being satisfied with small achievements.

Let me repeat, I am not recommending this as a way to run a life, merely as one that is useful in the daily rub of things.

Also miniature golf was tricky. You hit the ball into an aperture and some inner mechanism made it reappear in a spot where you weren't looking for it. I have found this to be a chastening lesson to absorb. Our endeavors do not always turn out the way we had expected. In miniature golf, as a matter of fact, quite the opposite. As a result of this early training I never expect things to go right. It has saved me a lot of fraying of the nerves and visceral perturbation.

When I drop a letter in the mailbox I am not distraught when it doesn't turn up where it is directed. On the contrary I am pleasantly surprised when it does so.

Carefully laid plans that do not go agley are for me a bonus. The miniature golf course was a hard taskmaster in this respect. Too often the pellet emerged from an unexpected hole. The man who accepts early on that this is the way life is likely to treat him may not live the most gorgeous of lives, but he is relatively immune to disappointment.

What else now? Vaudeville. From my earliest youth until this particular art form disappeared, I was a devotee of vaudeville. From it I gathered one important rule of life.

Eventually everybody gets tired of your act unless you change it once in a while.

I can think of very few other maxims as valuable for getting along in the world.

Better, in some ways, than attending a university is the habit of looking in store windows, which has been my life-long preoccupation. From looking in store windows a young man discovers all the variety of things in this world that he does not need. If it is the window of a pawnbroker he will get some feeling of the evanescence of fame and the fleeting nature of human ambition.

Looking in a store window is also the only way a man can tell whether his necktie is on straight without looking in a mirror which, until fairly recently, was regarded as unmanly.

Athletics molded me quite a bit. In running the hurdles, for example, I discovered the rule of conduct which stands a man in the best stead if he is to be employed by a giant corporation. It is that if you bob up and down quite a bit nobody will notice that you really have no talent for running.

Also if you see you have no possible chance of winning you can always fall over the last hurdle, leading everyone, or yourself at least, to get the impression that you would have finished first had it not been for that unfortunate accident.

In the track meet of life my suggestion is to go in for the hurdles and eschew the flat races which can make you look bad.

There were other influences, of course, but they will have to wait for the more expansive space of my three volume autobiography.

❖❖❖❖

The First Thanksgiving

Most of us have a pretty clear picture of the first Thanksgiving, or rather several pictures. One is of the Pilgrim fathers and mothers going to church through the snow. The men are carrying blunderbusses, if that is the plural I'm after. This was for protection from the Indians who were lurking in the forest. Incidentally, Indians always either lurked or skulked, and the difference between the two has puzzled many historians and students of the frontier. Actually, it was a matter of which tribes they belonged to. In New England, where the forests are composed of large and primeval trees, the Indians lurked. Skulking requires bending over farther than lurking and is therefore typical of the plains Indians, who had to hide behind bushes, clumps of grass, or highway signs.

On the first Thanksgiving the Indians lurked between the Pilgrims and the church. This made it very easy to get to church. You just walked between the Indians and there you were.

It is more difficult to get to church on Thanksgiving these days.

For some reason.

Another picture we all have is of a Pilgrim father coming home with a turkey over his shoulder and an arrow through his hat. It is a good thing that wild turkeys were indigenous to the neighborhood. Suppose, for example, it had been kangaroo country. Today, instead of turkeys, we would be eating roast kangaroo which, besides tasting terrible, lasts forever. We'd have kangaroo hash until Jefferson's birthday.

Now about the arrow in the hat. According to all the pictures, that is the only place where the Indians ever hit the Pilgrim fathers.

It is a good thing for us (and an even better thing for them) that the Pilgrims weren't about a foot taller. As it was, they had just enough room between the tops of their heads and the crowns of their hats to accommodate an arrow.

The Indians were puzzled quite a bit by the way they could put an arrow right through a Pilgrim's hat without seeming to bother the Pilgrim.

This was a big factor in the Indians' finally getting disgusted and selling out their eastern interests.

Well, as everybody knows, the Indians, after they tired of trying to shoot the Pilgrims and hitting nothing but their hats, accepted an invitation to dinner. Probably they wanted to get a closer look at those hats and count the holes.

Anyway, that's another picture we all have of the early Thanksgivings—the Indians sitting around and joining in the feast. The Indians in those days weren't very particular about what they ate, so they were much better guests than relatives and people like that who are always asking for white meat and complaining about lumps in the mashed potatoes.

Back in those times Thanksgiving feasts lasted all day, and the food was cooked exactly right, because people weren't always popping their heads in the kitchen and saying, "Get that junk on the table, for Pete's sake, or we'll miss the kickoff."

Another thing that happened on Thanksgiving was that John Alden proposed to Priscilla Mullens on behalf of Miles Standish, and just who was kidding anybody except Longfellow in that mix-up it's hard to say.

Anyway, that about rounds up everything that the average American knows about the first Thanksgiving.

❖❖❖❖

Self-Analysis

The way it is, you are talking on the telephone to a business acquaintance you have never met. You are visiting in his city. Hitherto you have only corresponded.

"Let us," he says, in modern business's most vivid phrase, "have lunch together."

You agree; he names a time and place.

Then comes the trouble.

"Uh, er," he says, "what do you look like?"

Who can describe himself? It should be easy. That face you have shaved every day for years should be as familiar as the back of your hand. More familiar, in fact. Did you ever know anybody who spent much time studying the back of his hand? Your height, weight, eye color—all the statistics—are on file with your doctor, the police, and at least one agency of the federal government.

But for purposes of instant recognition they aren't much help. Eyes Br., Hair Br., No Dist. Phys. Char. This doesn't add up to anything very distinctive.

Truman Capote once described himself as being as tall as a shotgun. A colorful phrase, but the chances are that you are taller than a shotgun and have no great desire to be mistaken for Truman Capote.

I have a friend who rises to the occasion by saying, "I look like that fellow in the newspaper—the unidentified companion of the slain woman."

He does, too. People have no trouble spotting him.

But it wouldn't work for most of us.

There are all sorts of pitfalls in this business. Suppose you have been generously endowed nasaly.

"You can tell me," you chuckle modestly, "by the great beak which will precede me by several feet as I enter the foyer."

Well, it turns out, if you have a cucumber of a nose, he has a watermelon. You are Durante; he is Cyrano.

Naturally he isn't going to recognize you by what seems to him like a nubbin of a nose. Furthermore, he is going to be skeptical of any business proposition you may advance. His feeling will be that a man who overstates the size of his nose will not shrink from misrepresentation in the fiscal field as well.

Or suppose you say, "I'm tall and thin."

One of two things happens. Either the man you are meeting is so much taller and thinner that you will seem short and fat by comparison or he will be so short and fat that he thinks everybody else is tall and thin and will spend fifteen minutes stopping the wrong people, thinking they are you.

The comparative ages of the men involved is also a factor. Suppose one says, "Well, my wife thinks I look like Milton Sills." If the other man is under fifty, this is no help at all. The reverse is when a younger man says, "My wife thinks I look like Robert Redford." Such a remark not only puzzles the older man but leads him to put the other down as an insolent young puppy.

The best solution may be the poetic approach: "Sam, I'll tell you frankly, mine is a face that was carved by the winds of adversity. The noble brow, not free from those lines which indicate intellectual activity, overhangs two piercing eyes, in which an expression of ineffable sadness is relieved by a twinkle of humor. The boldly aquiline nose hints of aristocratic forebears, while the determined jut of the chin—"

By this time, or even before, he is ready to give up.

"All right, all right," he yells. "Never mind what you look like. I'll be wearing a red bow tie and snowshoes."

DECEMBER

How to Decorate with Christmas Cards

I get awfully sick of harking back to the old days and how great they were, but it is a temptation, and if I may be allowed my last hark of 1962, may I ask if anyone remembers when you just put the Christmas cards in a pile on the table?

Oh, how primitive we were then, how backward. And how happy.

Now what we have to do is every year we have to think of a new, cute thing to do with the cards. If we have a mantelpiece, we do not set the cards up on the mantelpiece, festive though the effect may be. Our first year in a house with a mantelpiece we can get away with it. After that, it's been done, and some new effect must be strived for.

Also there is the worry about what the friends and neighbors are doing with their cards. The secret of seasonal decor is to be different.

You will find situations such as this:

Sam and Ethel Nevermind have hit upon a darling idea for their cards. They have affixed them with tape to the railing of the steps leading to the second floor. It has been a painstaking job, fraught with decisions such as whether an ugly card from an important friend should be more prominently displayed than a beautiful card from a nobody.

It is a Saturday impinging upon Christmas. Sam has added the day's take of cards to the railing, and is just stepping back to admire the effect when Ethel enters, sniffling.

"Take down the cards, Sam!" she cries.

"Wha—?"

"I have just returned from Susie Snavely's luncheon and you know where she and Norman had their Christmas cards?"

"Not—?"

"Too true," she continues, "taped to the railing. All the girls raved and gushed and said, 'How original,' and so on. Next week they come to our house.

"I will never be able to hold up my head in this town again if word gets around that we stuck our Christmas cards along the railing the way Susie Snavely did hers."

"We could move," Sam suggests. "I can ask the boss for a transfer to Des Moines."

"Not enough time," Ethel snaps, after a moment's reflection. "Take down the cards, Sam. We'll have to put them somewhere else."

They end up pinning them to the lampshades.

The challenge obviously increases as the years pass. I cite the case of a friend who said, "We have stood the cards on the mantelpiece, we have pasted them on mirrors, we have hung them on the tree and strung them on ribbons hanging from the ceiling.

"We have used them to paper the inside of the refrigerator, we have stuck them on the front door, and taped them on the windows. We have shaped them into trees and wreaths and Santas. One year, when a bunch of them came as early as Thanksgiving, we built them into the shape of a turkey.

"We have plastered them on the garage door, carpeted the

hall with them and had them floating around the house on balloons.

"This year we haven't even opened them. We're afraid to. The minute we open them we'll have to think up some new arrangement and, frankly, we're stumped.

"Have you noticed how more and more people every year are leaving town for Christmas, shutting up their houses and going to Florida or Arizona or some Caribbean island? It is not that they are nuts for sun and spray. They just can't face the problem of what to do with the cards.

"Little though I can afford it, my wife and I may have to join this flight to dodge the issue."

His expression was so sad that I made the supreme sacrifice.

"I'll tell you what," I said. "Here is an idea that may seem a little radical, but it's different. I guarantee that nobody in your set will have anything like it."

"Anything," he said. "Anything. I'll do it. What is it?"

"Well," I said, "you take all the cards and you pile them on the table."

He rushed off, a happy man. For my part, I turned apprehensively for home, wondering how I could tell my wife that we would have to do something else with our Christmas cards besides pile them on the table.

❖❖❖❖

Thoughts on Retirement

Another strange thing about the way we order our society is that people work in miserable, cold climates, then retire to balmy ones. This makes no sense whatever.

If we were to be at all rational, we would spend our working years in sun-drenched climes and retire to snow and ice.

The point about what generally is regarded to be bad weather is not that there is anything wrong with it of itself, but that you have to go to work through it, and home again through worse. If snow were to be avoided at all costs, there would be no winter sports industry, which we all know is an expanding one. People, some of whom you may know, will travel many miles to slide down a frozen hill, thus proving that snow is fun as long as you aren't working.

Catch a child and ask him. He will tell you that snow is neat or groovy or whatever word is currently replacing keen. The reason he feels this way is that getting out in the mess is optional on his part (especially when the situation gets so tricky that school is let out).

But his father, and very likely his mother, must defy the blizzard, regardless.

O.K., it's in the contract, and no big deal.

What I can't understand is why a man who battles this sort of existence for forty years or more slips away to a sunnier scene when it is no longer necessary for him to hack the travel back and forth to the job.

It seems to me to be a lovely picture: You get up early, prop your feet on the radiator, lean back with a cup of coffee, your pipe (a mild cigar for the Ms.) and observe the unretired rats going forth to join the rat race.

"Look, Maw, there's young Charlie Mumph, gouging away at his windshield. If I can read the smoke signals his breath is sending up he's cussing something scandalous."

"Hush, Paw," Maw giggles.

"Charlie's not a day over fifty-two; he's got thirteen more years of it. Go to it, Charlie. Attaboy."

"Oh, look," Maw says, "there is young Phoebe Ann Density, leaving one galosh in the snowdrift and hopping around like a chicken with its head off."

"Hee, hee," you chuckle, "and there goes her bus. Won't be another one for half an hour. Well, about time for Fred

Standstill from the filling station to come by to get some-body started. Yep, here he comes now. Just about on schedule. Think I'll have another cup of coffee before I go back to bed."

The poet advised living in a house by the side of the road. That is my ideal exactly. I would want one with a good view of the street, preferably overlooking a particularly nasty hill where cars tend to slide around and there is likely to be a great spinning of wheels. Nothing, I should think, would cheer the heart of the man who doesn't have to go anywhere like listening to the screech of other people burning the treads off their tires.

But not a house, preferably a second floor apartment, which gives a broader view and also removes the temptation (slim though it may be) to go out and shovel snow or help push a car.

Let us contrast this with someone who has retired to El Cucaracha Acres. He looks out the window and sees people going to work in their shirtsleeves and with their worst problem whether the air-conditioning in the car is working.

Envy is what eats us up in this world. So why retire some place where everybody you see outside your window is hav-ing a better time than you are? Take your leisure where the poor devils out there in the sleet and slush can look in and envy you.

If you want to play shuffleboard, there's the whole summer.

❖❖❖❖

The Xmas File

A recent magazine article, charging dissension among Santa Claus's top advisers, particularly involving the issue of a "hard" or "soft" policy on naughty children, is causing heated discussions of whether there is a "leak" in North Pole security.

The article, coauthored by two journalists known to have exceptionally close personal contacts within the Claus administration, described Edgar Elf, Secretary of Sugar Plums, as leader of the "polar bears," and Norbert Gnome, a former college roommate of Santa's, as the chief of the "reindeer."

The former group was said to have urged a strong stand against making compromises with the children of the world.

"If we let the kids get the idea that they can get away with being bad before Christmas and still get just as many toys, Santa Claus will be reduced to a second-rate power," a leading "polar bear" was quoted as saying.

The "reindeer," on the other hand, were represented as fearing that a tough policy in this regard could lead to retaliatory actions by the children and, even, all-out war.

Gnome, or someone close to him, is said to have phrased the question this way: "Suppose one of our reconnaissance sleighs is shot down? What do we do then? Go in with everything we have—switches and ashes in the stockings and only sturdy, sensible presents under the tree? Are we really prepared to stage a massive crunch if they start kicking our department store agents in the shin?"

During the crisis, Santa Claus is known to have met daily with his Executive Managers committee, a newly organized group which quickly picked up a typical North Pole nickname, XMas.

A member of XMas gave the authors this description of the situation: "We were standing in an eyeball-to-eyeball confrontation with the kids of all nations. Then the other fellow blinked."

This, according to the story, was on December 2, when a group of leaders in the children's bloc showed signs of weakening in their intransigence. They began helping Mom around the house, running errands and making their beds.

216

This development came, of course, after Santa Claus had taken the admittedly hazardous step of invoking a blockade against the smuggling of toys or presents into the homes of naughty children from other sources, such as parents, uncles, or aunts.

The blockade, according to the authors, was agreed upon by a consensus of XMas. Instead of "polar bears" and "reindeer," they say, Santa's inner circle were now all "polar deer" and "reinbears." A compromise, in other words, had been effected.

Realizing that their dangerous bluff had been called, the children's supreme council not only sent Santa Claus assurances that they would be good but agreed to twenty-four-hour surveillance.

Of course, as has been pointed out by close observers, this does not end the knotty naughty child problem, but there appears to be no sign of a major deterioration of the status quo in the foreseeable future.

Whether all the rooftop Santa-traps have actually been disassembled remains, for example, to be seen.

But the really intriguing questions are how the proceedings of the top-secret XMas, with its security-minded slogan "Do Not Open 'Til Christmas" were allowed to reach the ears of a favored segment of the press.

There is speculation that, because of his early "soft" position, Norbert Gnome is to be eased out.

Santa Claus has made public a letter to Gnome, praising his activities and expressing confidence in his advice.

But informed opinion is inclined to adopt a "wait-and-see" attitude.

❖❖❖❖

Speaking of Business

"Testing," said Delahanty, "1, 2, 3, 4. All right, this is a take on lunch, December 6. I'll have the hamburger, easy on the grease."

"What are you doing?" asked Rose, the waitress.

"It is always best to get a voice level on these things," said Delahanty. "What do you think about North Dakota?"

"I try not to think about it," said Rose. "Especially this time of year."

"We have a sales problem up there," said Delahanty, "and my thinking is that if we emphasize the 626-A model, backed by a strong advertising program, we may be able to recoup our third-quarter losses. Do you agree?"

"Should I?"

"It doesn't really matter," said Delahanty. "The point is I'm getting some good deductible conversation on the tape."

"What has brought this on?" asked Rose.

"The new expense account rules from the Internal Revenue service," said Delahanty, "A Chicago restaurant provides tape recorders for the customers so they can prove the luncheon can be deducted because business was discussed. Until the shortsighted management of this place gets around to it, I am bringing my own recorder with me."

"I wondered who that little fellow was," said Rose, "sitting on the table with the spools going round on his head. I hated to inquire. You have some strange-looking friends, you know."

As if this were their entrance cue, Phil Plimmer and Cromwell Boggs sat down at the table.

"Well," said Phil Plimmer, "it's a nice day."

"Do you mean," asked Delahanty, "from a retail or wholesale viewpoint, taking into account the well-known effects climate has upon consumer habits?"

"What is this?" asked Phil Plimmer.

"For the record, boy," said Delahanty. "The IRS has no desire to be picayune or anti-business, but I very much doubt if you would be very happy sitting there in the tax office after you have claimed this lunch as a business expense and the man is playing the tape and all you are saying is, 'It's a nice day.'"

"I was planning to say some other things, too," said Phil Plimmer.

"Enunciate more clearly," said Cromwell Boggs. "Delahanty is taping the whole thing so he can take it off his income tax."

"So we all can," said Delahanty, generously. "The thing to remember is—wait until I stop this tape for a minute—to make a business reference in everything you say. For example, don't just ask me how's the wife. Say something like, 'I understand Amalgamated is expanding into extruded aluminum how's the wife.'"

"What's extruded aluminum?" Plimmer inquired politely.

"She's fine, thanks, and wants Edna to call her so we could maybe get together some Saturday night and discuss the bridge business."

"Bridge business," chortled Cromwell Boggs. "That's an inspired touch, Delahanty. Now, Rose, I'd like the vegetable soup, keeping in mind that in my line of work I number the vegetable farmers of America among my possible customers and how can I deal with them effectively unless I eat their soup?"

"If you have a minute, fellow businessmen," cried Phil Plimmer, getting into the spirit of the thing, "I'd like to analyze some of the shows I saw on the teevy last night, from the standpoint of their impact upon our marketing methodology."

"Which one of you tycoons is picking up the check?" asked Rose.

"What do you mean?" replied Delahanty.

"It's not deductible unless somebody pays for the whole thing," Rose said.

"Separate checks," said all three at once, as Delahanty erased the tape.

❖❖❖❖

Dear Virginia

A little girl named Virginia, or someone writing in her name, wants to know if there is a Santa Claus. She says her friends tell her it is her daddy. She wants me to set her straight.

Why me?

I am a middle-aged curmudgeon who may or may not believe in either little girls or Santa Claus. I have the furnace to worry about and the cracked block on the car and the taxes, and I'm supposed to discuss the existence (or nonexistence) of Santa Claus with a little girl whose father may not even be a fan.

In order to get what might be a broader spectrum of opinion, I have passed this poignant inquiry on to others around the office and have received some replies, which I will send to Virginia without comment.

The writer of advice to the lovelorn:

"Listen, Sis, my word to you is to keep your nose out of other people's affairs. Santa Claus didn't ask me whether he exists or not, and I'll bet he didn't ask you either, so why don't you mind your own business? But all I can say is that a man who hangs around with a bunch of elves and goes flying off once a year in a sled and a red suit isn't mature.

"If either of you are real you need professional help, talk to your pastor or physician and send for my booklet, 'Living With Acne.'"

A sportswriter:

"Bill, don't get me involved in this. I am right in the middle of my annual hilarious column in which I suggest all sorts of funny gifts that Santa Claus might bring to sports celebs. I know you look forward to it as much as I do every year.

"You know the one, like where I suggest five more yards for that Atlanta player—I have to look up his name—who gained 995 yards this season. A major league shuffleboard franchise for Charles O. Finley. Two new knees and four more commercials for Broadway Joe. It's socko material, Bill, and brings in a lot of mail from the fans.

"So let's not make any waves about there not being any Santa Claus. If you think you have to quote me to this chick, you can say that there not only is a Santa Claus but that he is a pro all the way, has pride and class, and is one of the gentlemen of the game."

A militant Ms. reporter:

"Always glad to help a sister, Virginia. Let me tell you right off that if there is a Santa Claus you are better off not having anything to do with him.

"He is a sexist and a male chauvinist pig. Have your father (hah hah!) explain to you what that means. I'll give you a for instance. This person goes around bringing dolls to little girls and toy dump trucks to little boys. How about that for trying to force them into life-styles dictated by sexual politics?

"His wife is known as Mrs. Claus. Degrading. What was her maiden name? Has she no claim on an identity of her own? Virginia, I am enclosing a packet of informational literature on the subject of the sexual revolution which would do you a lot more good than worrying about such male-oriented trivia as Santa Claus. Come to the next meeting."

An editorial writer:

"Virginia, I'm glad you asked that question. Oddly enough another little girl named Virginia asked the same question of the *New York Sun* in 1897 and a wonderful editorial writer

221

named Francis Pharcellus Church wrote a dandy answer. I am sending you a copy. I don't know whether it did that other Virginia any good, but it was the greatest thing that ever happened to editorial writers. We just reprint it every year and get a whole afternoon off. Bless you, Pharcellus. Incidentally, that editorial first appeared on September 21. Virginia, can you tell me why that little girl was worrying about Santa Claus in September?"

If I can be of any further help to you, Ginny, drop me a line.

❖❖❖❖

S. Claus, Inc., Reels Under Fire from Title IX

You may recall a few years back when S. Claus, Inc., was accused of being an unfair employer because his hiring practices gave illegal preference to elves over gnomes. The whole situation became rather ugly for a while, but it has been settled now and things are fairly friendly in the backshop up there at the North Pole.

Now, however, an even more tender (not to say ticklish) problem has arisen. At this writing it does not appear that Christmas will have to be canceled, but it has been touch-and-go, with a little bump-and-run thrown in.

I refer, of couse, to accusations leveled by feminist groups accusing Santa Claus of being sexist. At first he misunderstood what he was being called, but even after it was explained to him, he still quivered with rage like a bowl full of jelly.

Briefly stated, and omitting the applicable federal statutes and judicial rulings cited, the gravamen of the case against Kris Kringle a.k.a. St. Nicholas d.b.a. Santa Claus, is that he is a male chauvinist pig because:

222

1. The work force in his toy shop is almost entirely masculine. While a few elf or gnome persons are employed they are limited mainly to the demeaning task of sewing doll clothes when, under Title IX, they should be allowed to pump up footballs.

2. No elf or gnome person occupies an executive position. The response of a spokesman for Claus that qualified elf and gnome persons could not be obtained and furthermore if they could they refused to work at the North Pole was brushed aside by the plaintiffs.

"If women can do brain transplants," said a spokesperson, "they can nail together wooden horsies."

The company's argument that nobody did brain transplants yet or nailed together wooden horses any more was labeled as irrelevant and self-serving.

3. Immediate affirmative action was called for to liberate Mrs. Claus who had been kept in a traditional position of subjugation to the culprit of the first part.

"All she is ever portrayed doing in the media or worse," the complaint alleges, "is darning S. Claus's socks or waiting up for him or baking cookies. She has been denied any opportunity for self-fulfillment."

The S. Claus personnel department said some consideration was once given to asking Mrs. Claus to ride shotgun on the sleigh but she had said, "Do you think I'm wacko? A person could get killed up there with those nutty reindeer. The old man made his bag—let him sleep in it."

Nevertheless, full freedom for Sister Claus to do her own thing is demanded whether she wants it or not.

4. And perhaps of most importance is the ongoing and apparently deliberate policy of S. Claus in giving out toys to good little boys and girls along lines which clearly define sex roles. (Whether it is discriminatory to give toys to good children to the exclusion of bad children and whether it is true that S. Claus does or does not maintain a notorious

blacklist of "bad" children, is a subject which may be gone into next year.)

Despite frequent warnings from concerned feminists S. Claus continues to deliver an unacceptable proportion of dolls to girls while giving more toy soldiers to boys.

Cease-and-desist orders are being sought on all the above complaints and if a consent decree is reached Christmas may proceed as usual. Whether little boys who get dolls can swap them with little girls who get toy soldiers is something they can work out between themselves.

❖❖❖❖❖

The Morning After

The morning after the Office Christmas party dawned cold and clear. It was even colder by 9:30, when Norman Skeam, a sub-junior executive at Flamboyant Products, Inc., entered the office he shared with three of his peers.

He made directly for the drinking fountain and went through the contortions required of a man who is trying to swallow an aspirin tablet with a faint jet of water as his only aid. It is a process which may have inspired the dance craze known as The Twist—at least the basic movement is the same.

Mary Plain, the stenographer whose desk was the fifth in the cubicle, looked up and giggled.

Norman Skeam walked to her desk, sat on a corner of it, and regarded her through eyes which he assumed to be open.

"Did I?" he asked, finally.

She giggled.

He groaned.

Miss Surrogate, personal secretary to Frank Flamboyant, president of Flamboyant Products, appeared through the door at the left. As she approached the desk where Mary Plain sat and Norman Skeam sagged, she detoured widely, then returned to her original course and disappeared through the door, right, marked "Office of the President." Norman Skeam's office, to be blunt about it, was more a corridor than anything else.

He looked at Mary Plain with eyes which were this time not only fully open but alive with anguished inquiry.

Mary Plain giggled again and nodded her head affirmatively.

Norman Skeam produced another groan and a one-syllable euphemism which disguised an inner despair.

The door to his employer's office opened and Miss Surrogate, holding a ballpoint pen aloft like the flaming sword of some avenging angel, announced, "Mr. Flamboyant would like to see you, Mr. Skeam. If you are not too busy."

The latter sentence was delivered with that sarcasm which Norman Skeam had once told her (at an earlier Office Christmas party, as a matter of fact) covered a basic immaturity.

After hastily straightening his tie and revisiting the drinking fountain, Norman Skeam found himself seated across a broad expanse of mahogany from his employer.

"Ah, Norman," said Mr. Flamboyant. "I want you to know how much I enjoyed our little talk at the Christmas party."

"Uh, yes, sir. Thank you," Norman ventured.

"Furthermore," said Mr. Flamboyant, poking at his desk blotter with a letter opener, "I want to say that I think all your suggestions were splendid. Would you care to expand upon one or two of them?"

"Well, Mr. Flamboyant, sir," Norman sid, "which one, or ones, did you have particularly in mind?"

"Which one did you like best?"

"Oh, well, sir, the one that, I think we discussed last," said

Norman, desperately trying to think what in the corporate world he had said to the old coot last night.

"Yes," said Mr. Flamboyant. "Let me see now—I had Miss Surrogate take some notes. That would be the one about lopping off dead wood at the top, I believe. I think something about senility was mentioned. 'A palsied hand at the wheel' was, I recall, one of your more telling phrases."

"Uh," commented Norman Skeam.

"Or perhaps," Mr. Flamboyant continued, "you would like to give us a few more facts on your Anchorage plan which I believe you referred to as Operation Frostbite."

"Well, sir, I'm not quite sure—"

"Of course you remember, Norman. This was the one which involved chartering a jet plane and flying all my sons-in-law, cousins, and nephews to Alaska to staff the branch office there."

"Uh, sir," said Norman Skeam, "I'm afraid I am a little unwell today. Could I, perhaps, finalize these matters in a later report?"

"Do that, Norman, my boy," said Mr. Flamboyant.

Norman Skeam, somehow or other, found his way out the door.

"You know," Mr. Flamboyant said to Miss Surrogate after he had left, "I don't think Norman was in his usual Christmas party form last night. His only really good point was Operation Frostbite and I can't remember when he said it."

"He didn't," said Miss Surrogate. "I just put it in my notes. Carried away, you might say, by the spirit of Christmas."

"Well," said Mr. Flamboyant, "bless us every one."

"Gesundheit," said Miss Surrogate.

❖❖❖❖

The Christmas Tree

"Ho! Ho! Ho!" a man may say, looking out at the snow and sleet and general subzeroness of the terrain. "It is a terrible night into which nobody but a nut would venture. It is a grand night for us to stay home whilst I read a fast snatch of Dickens in my mellow baritone and perhaps mull a little wine."

"Ho! Ho! Ho!" his wife will reply. "This is the ideal time to go out and buy a Christmas tree."

The man, being a veteran husband, should have known that it would work out this way. Women (or, more specifically, wives) prefer to buy the Christmas tree in the worst possible weather.

You will note that if November is mild, bachelors and single ladies will have their trees up and decorated long before the married people. They want to shop for the tree when the sun shines and the gale is restrained. This is because they have only themselves to please.

But not the wife.

For her the temperature should be well below freezing, the wind sharp. Precipitation is almost a must.

This scene ensues:

The family drives up to Friendly Fred's Tree Lot. The children are out of the car and away, scampering, as is childhood's wont, toward the most expensive section of the display.

"Come back here out of them magenta junipers, mauve spruces, and puce balsams," Dad bellows cheerily. "A plain green tree was good enough for John Wayne as a nipper and it's good enough for you."

Mother is poking around the trees.

"For Kris Kringle's sake," says Dad, "let's not poke at the trees, Grace. Let's get one and back to the cheery fire."

"Well, I don't know," says the wife. "I'm afraid that if we

227

get a tall one we don't have enough lights and if it's too small the children will be disappointed. On the other hand, the way our living room is now, since I moved the ormolu clock on the credenza, we need less of a horizontal accent than a vertical. So maybe we should strive for a tree that gives more of steeple-like effect of aspiring heavenward, than a bushy type that seems to shelter the family beneath its spreading boughs."

"I'm freezing," says Dad.

"When I was a girl," says the wife, "my father said he wouldn't give a pine house room, unless it was a Scotch pine. On the other hand, the balsam—"

"On the other hand," says Dad, "I have chilblains. Grab a tree. Any tree."

"Oh, you pick it, Sam," says Grace. "A man is naturally more woodsy than we frailer vessels. My father always picked the tree and Mumsy always said that a man was naturally more woodsy."

"Your father," says Sam, "was so woodsy that he was always shedding—tobacco, eye-glasses, lint. He was a very deciduous man, your father. Pick a tree. Come on, kids, Mother's found a tree. Let's go."

"Oh, I just can't make up my poor feminine mind," says the wife. "You pick one with your unerring masculine eye."

"O. K., all right," says Dad. "This one right here. Where's the man. Here's the money. Let's go before we're all lumps of ice."

The tree, as Mother shrewdly knew, is so ice encrusted, and frozen tight, that there is no chance of making an accurate appraisal of its conformation.

When carted home, with its tip bouncing jauntily outside the half-closed lid of the car trunk, the tree is conveyed to the basement. There it thaws. The limbs relax. What is revealed is the most unshapely tree that ever grew. Had he an opportunity to look at it, Joyce Kilmer would have revised his

228

opinion as to who makes trees.

The wife is, of course, ecstatic. It is her Christmas wish come true—a spavined, graceless tree, picked out by her husband.

"Oh, yes you did, Sam," she says if he protests. Then, turning to assembled neighbors, she expands. "Honestly, that man. This was the tree he had to have. Nothing else would do. I told him we ought to look around a little or at least have the man spread out the limbs. But, no, Mr. Know-it-all, Mr. Evergreen Expert, Mr. Forestry of 1962, he says, 'This is the one. A tree in a million.' I'd say it's a tree in a billion. If, that is, it's a tree."

All very funny and Ho! Ho! Ho! Here is a man who was only interested in getting his little brood off of Friendly Fred's frozen tundra. Now he has to take the ridicule and obloquy of having picked out a punk tree.

But it may be that he has not come out too badly at that. The wife is happy. She hums as she goes about the task of decorating the tree, showing what her artsy-craftiness can do to rehabilitate her husband's arboreal error. The kids, of course, think any tree is great. Happiness reigns in the home. It may be that everybody knew what he was doing all along.

❖❖❖❖

And You Thought You'd Rather Be in Palm Springs

While skiing, tobogganing, and schussing among the Giant Slaloms and other wild beasts are in progress in some parts of the country, others are offering lolling, surfing, and similar aquatic pursuits.

People who have been lured to these spots by costly publicity campaigns are missing out on the Slushorama of the Middle West.

It may be just as well since the novice, the slush-bunny as she or he may be called, can be embarrassed by her (or his) ignorance of slush. There is, for one thing, the tendency to denigrate slush as bad snow or wet sunshine. This sort of approach to slush is unacceptable. It must be judged for what it is, which is slush.

Do not say that this is rotten snow into which I have just stepped. Hold to the thought, rather, that it is outstanding slush.

Too often Middle Westerners hear ill-informed people step off the plane, bus, or whatever is running this time of year and exclaim: "Ecch! There is nothing to smite the eyebone but slush, eternal vistas of same."

The same persons do not arrive at Bad Salzburg or Palm Springs and complain that there is nothing visible but snow or sunshine. Instead they are ecstatic about the oversupply of both.

They should not despair. A few days in slush country and they will learn the thrills that come with being wise in the ways of slush.

At first they may expect to be the objects of good-natured derision. When standing on the sidewalk when a car drives by, spraying slush, they may retreat like a dropback quarterback, mincing backward, while making brushing gestures with the forearms. To give them their due, it was once done this way, and if they are old enough they may have seen this sort of performance in the newsreel.

With only a modicum of practice, however, they will learn to adopt the modern, or roll out, style. This improvement upon standard techniques was introduced in the late fifties by a group of young and innovative slush-folk in the Minneapolis area.

It involves a pivot on the right (or left, if it feels more comfortable) foot, turning the back on the street, for a quick dash to the nearest property line. It is more graceful and, at the same time, more dignified than the earlier method of backing up.

Business establishments are enlivened during slushy weather by discussions between those who still cling to the older tradition of backing away from slush and advocates of the newer turn and run method.

A man's generation can be pretty well established by whether it is the front of his overcoat or the back that is plastered with the effluvium from the gutters. And let it not be forgotten that it is those motorists, entering wholeheartedly into the spirit of the fun by driving through the biggest slush lagoons at forty miles an hour, who make the sport possible, even though they are seldom mentioned in the headlines.

The newcomer to slush can be identified at street intersections by the delicate way in which he attempts to pick his way among the hillocks. It is very much like trying to go off a ski jump an inch at a time.

Veterans of slush forge briskly ahead, often with a sensational leap which brings them down in a knee-deep pool of semiliquid muck. They realize that sooner or later the slush is going to get them.

There is a fatalistic mystique involved.

"Nobody mocks slush," hardened old-timers will tell you.

And so those who have grown up with slush welcome new addicts to the fold. Building an affinity with slush, learning to know its vagaries and to read its mysterious purposes, is a difficult task.

But it has its reward. He who has learned to live with slush will never again be satisfied with such pale substitutes as snow or sunshine.

Slush lives!

❖❖❖❖

Touching Bottom

It is clever planning that arranges for the year to hit bottom during the week before Christmas. The thinking behind this arrangement is that nobody will notice it.

In the rush of presents unwrapped, unmailed, and indeed, unbought, of cards unaddressed, of turkeys unthawed, of Christmas trees undecorated, and of children undisciplined, who has time to worry about the winter solstice?

Many people have speculated about the shape of the year. There are differing pictures. But everyone, I suppose, agrees that it isn't shaped like a circle. There is nothing even about it; there are hills and valleys, pimples and dimples. Time does not circle; it lurches.

And the bottom, the low point, is December 21, the shortest day, the longest night.

This is the time when the mysterious mechanism of the stars and planets is on dead center. Everything sort of sticks for a moment, until some majestic foot gives it a kick and it starts percolating again.

These are the days when you arise in darkness and come home from work in darkness. It is the time when the man who goes out for the paper in the morning looks down the black street and sees the occasional light from kitchens and bedrooms.

When the dawn comes, it comes reluctantly, as though it would make the day even shorter than its already pitifully few hours.

On its face, this is not a pleasant time, but it has its compensations. The city is a good place to be during the pre-Christmas week. When the dark comes early, the homeward-bound city-dweller is struck by the beauty of the lights, the mystery of the dusk.

People, dimly seen, seem to be intent on errands of interest and importance, even of romance. The passengers on the bus

232

are closer together, because the vehicle in which they ride is a moving oasis of light in the gloom.

And, more important, there is the fact that because the year has hit bottom, it is on its way back up. The end has been reached, the cold waters of winter have closed over our heads, but now our toes touch the bottom and we have flexed our knees to shoot up again toward the sunlight.

If the days are short, we know that they are getting longer.

The difference, day by day, may be imperceptible, but at least we know that we are moving in the right direction. However vague the glimmer, sunshine and the spring lie ahead.

It is still a long way off, however, and even the most optimistic of philosophers is grateful for the excitements of Christmas in this dark week. It is a time when we need all the gaiety we can get.

The diversions of Christmas enable us to look back upon the nadir of the year and say to ourselves, "Well, it wasn't so bad after all." We hardly noticed it, and now we are on the upswing.

All of us feel that way, that is, except for those who insist that the morning of New Year's Day is the lowest point of any year. For them we have no consolation—just sympathy.

❖❖❖❖❖

A Christmas Story

"Tell me a story of Christmas," she said. The television mumbled faint inanities in the next room. From a few houses down the block came the sound of car doors slamming and guests being greeted with large cordiality.

Her father thought awhile. His mind went back over the interminable parade of Christmas books he had read at the

233

bedsides of his children.

"Well," he started, tentatively, "once upon a time it was the week before Christmas, and all the little elves at the North Pole were sad—"

"I'm tired of elves," she whispered. And he could tell she was tired, maybe almost as weary as he was himself after the last few feverish days.

"O.K.," he said. "There was once, in a city not very far from here, the cutest wriggly little puppy you ever saw. The snow was falling, and this little puppy didn't have a home. As he walked along the streets, he saw a house which looked quite a bit like our house. And at the window—"

"Was a little girl who looked quite a bit like me," she sighed. "I'm tired of puppies. I love Pinky, of course. I mean story puppies."

"O.K.," he said. "No puppies. This narrows the field."

"What?"

"Nothing. I'll think of something. Oh, sure. There was a forest, way up in the North, farther even than where Uncle Ed lives. And all the trees were talking about how each one was going to be the grandest Christmas tree of all. One said, 'I'm going to stand in front of the White House where the President of the whole United States lives, and everybody will see me.'

"And another beautiful tree said, proudly, 'I am going to be in the middle of New York City and all the people will see me and think I am the most beautiful tree in the world.'

"And then a little fir tree spoke up and said, 'I am going to be a Christmas tree, too.' And all the trees laughed and laughed and said, 'A Christmas tree? You? Who would want you?'"

"No trees, Daddy," she said. "We have a tree at school and at Sunday school and at the supermarket and downstairs and a little one in my room. I am very tired of trees."

"You are very spoiled," he said.

234

"Hmmm," she replied. "Tell me a Christmas story."

"Let's see. All the reindeer up at the North Pole were looking forward to pulling Santa's sleigh. All but one; and he felt sad because," he began with a jolly ring in his voice, but quickly realized that this wasn't going to work either. His daughter didn't say anything; she just looked at him reproachfully.

"Tired of reindeer, too?" he asked. "Frankly, so am I. How about Christmas on the farm when I was a little boy? Would you like to hear about how it was in the olden days, when my grandfather would heat up bricks and put them in the sleigh and we'd all go for a ride?"

"Yes, Daddy," she said, obediently. "But not right now. Not tonight."

He was silent, thinking. His repertoire, he was afraid, was exhausted. She was quiet too. Maybe, he thought, I'm home free. Maybe she has gone to sleep.

"Daddy," she murmured. "Tell me a story of Christmas."

Then it was as though he could read the words, so firmly were they in his memory. Still holding her hand, he leaned back:

"'And it came to pass in those days, that there went out a decree from Caesar Augustus, that all the world should be taxed. . . . .'"

Her hand tightened a bit in his and he told her a Story of Christmas.